Making Educational
Psychology Work

This book is part of the Goodyear Series in Education, Theodore W. Hipple, University of Florida, Editor.

OTHER GOODYEAR BOOKS IN GENERAL METHODS AND CENTERS

AH HAH! The Inquiry Process of Generating and Testing Knowledge
John McCollum

A CALENDAR OF HOME/SCHOOL ACTIVITIES
Jo Anne Patricia Brosnahan and Barbara Walters Milne

CHANGE FOR CHILDREN Ideas and Activities for Individualizing Learning
Sandra N. Kaplan, Jo Ann B. Kaplan, Sheila K. Madsen, Bette K. Taylor

CREATING A LEARNING ENVIRONMENT A Learning Center Handbook
Ethel Breyfogle, Susan Nelson, Carol Pitts, Pamela Santich

THE LEARNING CENTER BOOK An Integrated Approach
Tom Davidson, Phyllis Fountain, Rachel Grogan, Verl Short, Judy Steely,
Katherine Freeman

ONE AT A TIME ALL AT ONCE The Creative Teacher's Guide to Individualized
Instruction Without Anarchy
Jack E. Blackburn and W. Conrad Powell

OPEN SESAME A Primer in Open Education
Evelyn M. Carswell and Darrell L. Roubinek

THE OTHER SIDE OF THE REPORT CARD A How-to-Do-It Program for
Affective Education
Larry Chase

THE TEACHER'S CHOICE
Sandra N. Kaplan, Sheila K. Madsen, Bette T. Gould

TEACHING FOR LEARNING Applying Educational Psychology in the Classroom
Myron H. Dembo

OTHER WAYS, OTHER MEANS Altered Awareness Activities for
Receptive Learning
Alton Harrison and Diann Musial

WILL THE REAL TEACHER PLEASE STAND UP? A Primer in Humanistic
Education, 2nd Edition
Mary Greer and Bonnie Rubinstein

A YOUNG CHILD EXPERIENCES Activities for Teaching and Learning
Sandra N. Kaplan, Jo Ann B. Kaplan, Sheila K. Madsen, Bette T. Gould

For information about these, or Goodyear books in Language Arts, Reading,
Science, Math, and Social Studies, write to:

Janet Jackson
Goodyear Publishing Company
1640 Fifth Street
Santa Monica, CA 90401
(213) 393-6731

MAKING EDUCATIONAL PSYCHOLOGY WORK

CARRYING CONCEPTS INTO ACTION

Beth Sulzer-Azaroff, Ph.D.
University of Massachusetts, Amherst

Judy McKinley Brewer, Ph.D.
Mansfield Day Treatment Center

Linda Ford
First Few Steps, Inc.
Greenfield, Massachusetts

Goodyear Publishing Company, Inc.
Santa Monica, California

Library of Congress Cataloging in Publication Data

Sulzer-Azaroff, Beth.
    Making educational psychology work.

    1. Educational psychology. I. Brewer, Judy
McKinley, joint author. II. Ford, Linda, joint author.
III. Title.
LB1051.S86   370.15   78-267
ISBN 0-87620-740-9

Library of Congress Catalog Card Number: 78-267
ISBN: 0-87620-740-9   Y-7409-9

Current Printing (last number):
10 9 8 7 6 5 4 3 2 1

Text and Cover Design: Christy Butterfield
Text and Cover Illustrations: Patrick Maloney
Technical Illustrations: Brenda Tighe

Printed in the United States of America

ACKNOWLEDGMENTS

We wish to express our appreciation to the hundreds of students and many proctors and instructors who have field tested this material and provided us with valuable feedback. We also appreciate the cooperation of the many school systems and service agencies that provided an environment conducive to students' use of these materials as they acquired educational psychology skills.

Particular thanks is deserved by the members of our families who have provided us with much emotional support and encouragement. We especially appreciate Leonid V. Azaroff's cleverness in providing the title *Making Educational Psychology Work*.

We also wish to thank Joan Baron, for her help in collecting source materials on measurement and evaluation, and Michele Thieberg, for her annotations to the Selected Readings and References.

Funding for the evaluation of this material was provided by the University of Massachusetts Center for Instructional Resources and Improvement. Such tangible encouragement has allowed us to provide students with a text that has been empirically tested, revised, and retested until it has demonstrated its ability to teach educational psychology cognitive and applied skills effectively and to merit high student satisfaction ratings. For this, we are all extremely appreciative.

CONTENTS

INTRODUCTION   1

ACTIVITY 1   Educational Goals and Instructional Objectives 7

Integrating principles of instructional technology; applying the result to the selection of instructional objectives

ACTIVITY 2   Analyzing Component Subtasks 21

Integrating instructional systems with theories of psychomotor, social, affective, and cognitive functioning; applying the result to the identification and selection of relevant tasks

ACTIVITY 3   Entering Behaviors and Other Prerequisite Behaviors 35

Integrating theories of human development and principles of behavior; applying the result to an analysis of the repertoire of individual students

ACTIVITY 4   Record Keeping, Feedback, and Avoiding and Coping with Problem Behaviors 53

Integrating theories of learning and principles of behavior; applying the result in motivating students and coping with problem behaviors

ACTIVITY 5   Designing an Instructional Sequence 73

Integrating theories of learning, models of teaching, and principles of behavior; applying the result to design effective instruction

Format 5.1. General Format for Developing an Instructional Sequence
Format 5.2. Programmed-Instruction Format
Format 5.3. Discussion Format
Format 5.4. Laboratory Format (Problem-Solving Format)
Format 5.5. On-Site Format
Format 5.6. Student-Designed Format

ACTIVITY 6   Evaluation, Revision, and Implementation 125

Integrating theories of tests and measurements with observational systems; applying the result to designing and conducting a sound evaluation of instruction

INTRODUCTION

This book of field activities is designed for students of educational psychology and related fields. By integrating the current theoretical and technological emphases in educational psychology, it should assist students to improve their instructional skills. We assume that the student who completes the activities is planning to engage in professional instruction, primarily in the formal instruction of the classroom. Instruction may also take place in many other situations, and includes in-service vocational training; instruction of special populations, such as institutionalized disabled persons; speech and language therapy; physical-rehabilitation training; and instruction in the home, as parents teach their children self-help, social, play, and other skills. Students who plan to use their instructional skills in one of these latter situations will still find the model presented here valuable as a frame of reference. Under such circumstances, however, the material should be modified by you, the student, to meet your own special requirements.

Regardless of your professional situation, you will want to be an effective and challenging instructor. But you may wonder just how you should begin to go about it. You have, no doubt, been exposed to a multitude of psychological theories, principles, and research "facts" that seem as though they would be useful in your instruction. Making the bridge between the rules and their application, however, can be extremely difficult. We hope to make this task a little easier.

This book provides practical experience in the development of effective instructional sequences, using a strategy we call the *general instructional model*. The general instructional model is a simple plan that combines psychological theory and principles with educational technology, and applies this combination in a step-by-step manner—first to achieve carefully defined educational goals, and later to evaluate the effectiveness of instruction. Figure 1 is a flow chart showing the sequencing and interrelation of activities in the model. As you can see, when you have successfully completed all the activities you should be able to perform the component tasks that result in effective instructional planning.*

You might wonder whether by simply reading through this book without completing the activities you could glean its benefits, thus saving your-

---

*Our presentation of the general instructional model is adapted from R. C. Anderson and G. W. Faust, *Educational Psychology: The Science of Instruction and Learning* (New York: Dodd, Mead & Co., 1973), pp. 13–55.

Figure 1 *The major components of the general instructional model. (Adapted with permission from Anderson and Faust,* Educational Psychology, *p. 170.)*

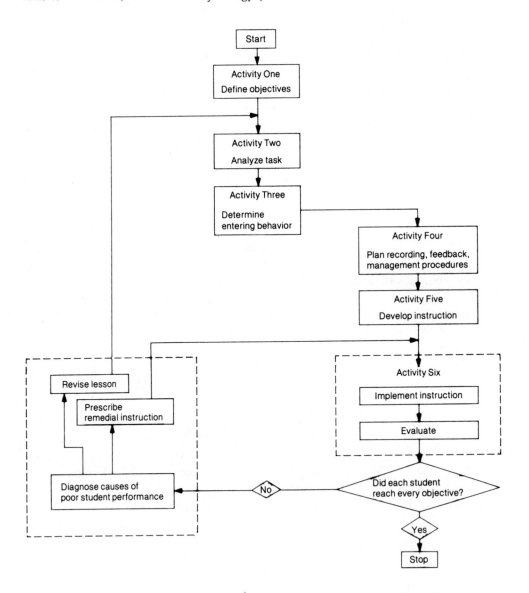

self much effort. We can only remind you that there is no substitute for real application. Should the resources be available, we'd particularly like to encourage you to work through the activities with actual students. If you perform the activities, you will be able to do much more than repeat instructional rules by rote. You will have *practiced* a set of the basic procedures that contribute to effective instruction. You will have acquired a new set of *behaviors* that will be directly useful to you in the future. If you test the material with students, they will profit by learning something new—and you will be able to assess the effectiveness of your material. Your newly acquired skills will be better retained and you'll be more likely to continue using them after your experience with this book is over.

The book is organized into a series of activities that help you to integrate the theories and principles of educational psychology and apply them to actual instruction, a few at a time. Each activity is based on those that went before, so you should complete them in order the first time through. You will probably want to return to the book once in a while to refresh your memory; at that time, you can select the activities you need and review them separately.

Activity 1 is based on the principle that the most effective and efficient instruction is *goal directed*. It integrates the rules for specifying goals and objectives that you have probably encountered in reading your course assignments. This activity will help you apply those rules; you will clarify educational goals (goals into which the students should have had some input) by defining them in precise, observable terms. You will describe specifically what your students are to *do* in order to demonstrate the learning toward which your instruction is directed, restating the goals as *instructional objectives*. The educational goals—statements of broad goals and values—are translated into specific performances, conditions, and standards or criteria.

Many theorists in educational psychology have devoted themselves to the continual refinement of the analysis of human functioning. Attention has been focused on various categories of functioning: physical or psychomotor, emotional or affective, social, and intellectual or cognitive. In the second activity you will have the opportunity to integrate the theories you have studied and apply them to the analysis and selection of relevant and sophisticated tasks. Activity 2 also integrates various systems of instructional planning. You are given practice in applying the systems approach to instructional planning by being asked to analyze the component tasks—the intermediate skills and knowledge—that will be required for the students to achieve the instructional objectives you have described. This activity is called a *task analysis*.

Activity 3 deals with *entering behaviors*, the behaviors that are already part of the students' repertoires just prior to instruction. You will decide which behaviors students must have in their repertoires for your planned instruction to be effective, and how to adapt your instruction to the variation that always exists among students in a group. This sequence of steps should incorporate the recent knowledge derived from theorists and researchers in human development and social learning. You will find yourself referring to the textual material you've read, such as Piaget's theories of cognitive development, Bandura's social-learning theories, and Bijou's functional analysis of child development. This information will help you to match your planning more realistically to your students' capabilities. Finally, you will consider each student in your class as an individual and plan instructional adjustments to allow for differences in your students' entering behaviors.

In the fourth activity, you will learn how to design record-keeping systems: how to develop a system that clearly shows each student the progress made towards reaching the objectives. You will also begin to evaluate general procedures for providing reinforcing and corrective feedback. The procedures are derived from the literature of learning theory and behavior analysis and are also applicable to planning to be undertaken to avoid or cope with behavior problems.

The fifth activity gives you the opportunity to take the various teaching models, behavior principles, and learning theories you have encountered in your reading and apply them in a meaningful way. You will select, design, and organize all the materials and procedures to be used in your instruction. Flexibility is incorporated into this activity through the provision of various alternative instructional formats—some selected by the students, some by the teacher—plus a number of other activities you can plan by yourself.

The sixth activity allows you to implement the instruction you have developed and to evaluate its effectiveness in reaching the prespecified objectives. Test and measurement theory, student observation, and the analysis of teacher-student interaction provide the framework for this activity. By translating them into action, abstract concepts become more meaningful.

From the first activity to the last, you will be working on the development of a single instructional sequence, an instructional episode that takes place during a single period of instructional time. The first time through the model, developing this sequence will require some effort and a fairly large investment of time, for you will need to refresh your knowledge of the content of your study as you begin to apply it. However, you will gradually become more and more skilled as you design each of the components. When you are finished, the outline of the general instructional model at the end of the book should provide a structure for future instruction. If you invest the time, your teaching effectiveness should be enhanced. If you are, or are going to be, a serious teacher, instructional effectiveness is a crucial aspect of your performance.

As you use this book:

- Begin by skimming through the entire book. Try to conceptualize the entire procedure and how each activity builds upon previous ones.

- Before you start each activity, read it through carefully. You should be aware of the steps following each task you perform and of how the products of your efforts will be used later. Pay special attention to any criteria checklists that follow the tasks, as they help you and your instructor (or proctor) evaluate your product.

- Refresh your memory of the content of your studies that pertain to each activity. By checking the Suggested Readings at the end of an activity or by checking with your instructor, you should be able to locate the appropriate material for review.

The objective of this book can be stated as follows:

For a topic of your choice and using the outline provided at the end of this book, you should be able to properly construct, administer, and evaluate an instructional sequence in the systematic manner described as the *general instructional model*.

1

EDUCATIONAL GOALS AND INSTRUCTIONAL OBJECTIVES

Objectives

Assuming that you have already mastered some basic textual material on instructional-technology goals and objectives, on completing this activity you should be able to:

- Write an array (three to nine) of educational goals.

- Define *challenging, interesting,* and *relevant* in this context and write at least three educational goals having each of these characteristics.

- Select one educational goal that has all three characteristics.

- Define *instructional objective,* including three essential components.

- Identify each of the essential components of an instructional objective in sample objectives.

- Refine or redefine vague criteria by using a sorting system. Refined criteria should appear more objective to your instructor than the original criteria.

- Write five instructional objectives related to a selected educational goal. All the essential components of an instructional objective should be included.

(Not all objectives included in the text contain a standard or criterion, since occasionally the standard is so obvious that it is in effect "built in" to the objective itself.)

Educational Goals and Instructional Objectives

Effective education, like many other human endeavors, is goal directed. When architects design a building, they must first know the function it is to perform. When we plan a trip, we first select the destination, then consider various routes to reach it. Selecting alternative learning activities for instructional planning will likewise be most effective when the goals of education are first carefully delineated. This first field activity is designed to help you focus on specific educational goals, thereby enabling you to begin to chart an instructional course. You will ultimately select a sample educational goal, and then develop instructional objectives that will lead toward that goal.

Selecting Sample Educational Goals

In this section you will be asked to select some sample educational goals. These will help you focus your plans for teaching a lesson. Since these field activities will entail an investment of time and effort, the educational goals towards which they are directed should be challenging, interesting, and relevant for you and for the students you plan to teach. (Terms for the persons served, such as *client, trainee, child,* or *resident,* may be substituted for *student* where appropriate throughout this book.)

To find a *challenging* goal, think in broad terms about a goal that will encompass many varied learning activities:

- The student should learn to make purchases and to verify receiving the correct change.

- The student should learn about the impact of industrialization upon the major social and political systems in the nation.

- The student should become sufficiently familiar with the various stages in the history of music that a fuller appreciation of individual compositions results.

- The student should learn to make furniture (or ceramic pieces, or to draw electronic circuits).

- The student should learn appropriate behaviors for social activities in the community.

- The student should learn to swim (or operate a sailboat, or play football, or engage in competitive gymnastics).

List three educational goals that you think would encompass many varied learning activities and would therefore be *challenging* to you and your students.

1.1 _____

_____

1.2 _____

_____

1.3 _____

_____

Identifying an *interesting* goal is a fairly subjective activity. You need to be thoroughly familiar with your students and yourself. Identify some educational goals that sound exciting to you and that you think would really "turn on" your students. To get ideas you might try the following:

- Think about some of the most exciting aspects of your own school experiences.

- Look through school catalogs and curriculum guides in the library.

- Survey texts on curriculum and instruction, for example, on teaching reading, music, or social studies.

- Interview teachers and ask them what they are trying to accomplish with their students.

- Ask your instructor in this course to arrange a school observation for you.

- Talk to your professors and friends.

Now list three educational goals that you feel would be *interesting* to you and your students. (These may be the same as 1.1, 1.2, and 1.3, or they may be different.)

1.4 _____

_____

1.5 _____

_____

1.6 _____

_____

The educational goal that you select should be *relevant* both to you and to your students. That is, engaging in field activities directed towards this goal should enhance both your and their behavioral repertoires. They should enable you both to accomplish related activities in the future. You should have a meaningful and constructive purpose in mind.

List three educational goals that are *relevant* for you and your students. Tell why you feel each is relevant. (You may repeat earlier goals if appropriate.)

1.7 a. Goal _____

_____

b. Relevance for you _____

_____

c. Relevance for your students _____

_____

1.8 a. Goal _____

_____

b. Relevance for you _____

_____

c. Relevance for your students _____

_____

1.9 a. Goal _____

_____

b. Relevance for you _____

_____

c. Relevance for your students _____

_____

At this point you have an array of goals; select *one*. That goal should meet all three of the preceding criteria and should be one that you want to serve as a focus for the ten-minute to two-hour lesson you will develop later. Write the goal here:

1.10 _____

_____

_____

Instructional Objectives

Having used a logical process to select an educational goal, you are now ready to begin to map out alternative activities for achieving that goal. We are going to ask that these be specified in the form of *instructional objectives:* full-sentence descriptions of what the student should be able to do upon the completion of instruction, expressed as specific observable behaviors, and using an action verb. The advantages of such statements include clarity of purpose, ease of communication, objectivity, and their usefulness as a groundwork for later evaluation.

Instructional objectives contain three major properties. First, the observable behaviors, expressed in action verbs, can be *measured*—for example, number of times correct (frequency); number of times correct within a total number of opportunities × 100 (percentage); "types twenty words per minute" (rate); or "swims freestyle for a given period of time" (duration). Second, the particular *conditions* under which the behavior is expected to occur are specified: where, when, with whose help, or with what materials or other "givens." For example, "Having access to the library, the student should———"; "Given a dry track and winds of less than———"; "Without referring to books, notes, or a calculator, the student———"; "Given a potter's wheel and clay of proper consistency for throwing,———." (Occasionally the conditions are *so* obvious that they may be omitted—for example, "Given a shoe with a lace, the child should be able to tie a bow that remains tied for at least one half hour." The condition "Given a shoe with a lace" could be omitted.) The third major property of an instructional objective is a *standard* or *criterion* of acceptable performance. Some examples include: "90 percent for three days in a row"; "for at least thirty minutes without stopping"; and "judged acceptable according to a predetermined set of criteria." (Occasionally the standard is so obvious that it may be omitted: "The student flying solo should be able to land the plane safely every time.")

Here are some illustrative instructional objectives for the sample educational goals listed earlier:

Using a simulated general store and play money, the student should be able to purchase an item and verify receiving the correct change by (writing the sum) of the cost of the item plus the change to yield the original amount, at least nine times out of ten.

As you look at this objective, you will notice a number of verb phrases. One is circled—writing the sum, since it includes an action verb that can be objectively measured (correct frequency, proportion, or percentage of times), the first major component of an instructional objective.

1.11   For the following instructional objective, find and circle the measurable action verb phrase:

Using the library as a resource, the student should be able to make an oral presentation summarizing legal decisions related to post–Civil War industrial development. At least three relevant legal decisions should be discussed and their sources appropriately cited.

You have probably noticed that parts of the two objectives are underlined. These, of course, indicate the *conditions* under which the response is expected to occur.

1.12   In the next objective, draw a line under the conditions under which the response is expected to occur:

After listening to a brief selection of taped music, the student should (identify in writing) the historical period to which it belongs, and be correct at least eight times out of ten trials.

1.13   The significance of the wavy line should be obvious to you. It indicates the _____

1.14   Here is an instructional objective. Identify the standard or criterion for minimal acceptability by drawing a wavy line beneath it:

The student should construct a circuit for sending Morse Code messages from a printed wiring diagram, to the instructor's satisfaction.

1.15   Draw a wavy line beneath the statement of the standard or criterion of acceptability:

The student should use acceptable table manners in a restaurant.

You were probably a little concerned because the term acceptable (the correct answer) is somewhat subjective. What may be acceptable by one person's standards may not be acceptable by another's. You are right to conclude that the criterion should be stated more objectively. This is also true of the criterion under 1.14—to the "satisfaction" of the instructor. If your instructional objective includes such ambiguous criteria, you should try to refine or redefine them.

We could redefine "to the instructor's satisfaction" by substituting "demonstrating its operation by transmitting five Morse Code letters for the instructor."

1.16 Take the phrase "acceptable table manners" and refine it by stating some of its objective, observable components.

a. Takes bites no larger than one-half inch square, nine times out of ten.

b. _____

c. _____

Here is another criterion that might be difficult to define:

The student should do graceful floor exercises.

Again graceful is a subjective term. Refining or redefining it may prove difficult. In his book *Goal Analysis*, Mager makes a useful suggestion. Many instances of the acceptable and many of the not acceptable should be sorted into two piles; one should then ask what was the basis for the sorting.* Taking the term "graceful," the sorting might look like this:

Graceful

Acceptable	Not Acceptable
Smooth transitions from one movement to another	Pauses between movements
Never trips or stumbles	Trips or stumbles

Many others could be added.

*R. F. Mager, *Goal Analysis* (Belmont, Ca.: Fearon Publishers, 1972), p. 43.

Because we would like to encourage you to teach subtle or sophisticated behaviors, and because the criteria for the acceptability of such behaviors are frequently difficult to define, we would like you to practice a bit. Here's a difficult one:

The student should be able to craft a <u>tasteful</u> object.

1.17   Think of objects with which you are familiar, such as crafts, clothing, works of art, or furnishings, and mentally (or even physically) sort them into "tasteful" and "tasteless" piles. List below a few of the criteria you found yourself using as standards to do the sorting.

Object Category _____ (for example, clothing)

Tasteful	Criterion	Tasteless	Criterion
(for example, simple)	(one ornament or less)	(flamboyant)	(more than three ornaments)

1.18 Now suggest a vague criterion term of your own (such as "beautiful," "creative," or "sophisticated") and apply it to a person or an object (for example, "creative poet"). Then repeat the process of 1.17.

Object or Person ＿＿＿＿＿＿ (for example, poet)

Your
Term: ＿＿＿＿＿
(Example: creative)

Your
Term: ＿＿＿＿＿
(uncreative)

Term	Criterion	Term	Criterion
(for example, original use of metaphor)	(not used by others)	(unoriginal use of metaphor)	(used frequently in poems)
＿＿＿＿＿	＿＿＿＿＿	＿＿＿＿＿	＿＿＿＿＿
＿＿＿＿＿	＿＿＿＿＿	＿＿＿＿＿	＿＿＿＿＿
＿＿＿＿＿	＿＿＿＿＿	＿＿＿＿＿	＿＿＿＿＿
＿＿＿＿＿	＿＿＿＿＿	＿＿＿＿＿	＿＿＿＿＿

1.19 At this point you should be ready to write some instructional objectives of your own. Referring to your educational goal (1.10), write five (or more) related instructional objectives that you would like your student(s) to accomplish.

a. ＿＿＿＿＿＿＿＿＿＿＿＿＿＿＿＿＿＿＿＿

＿＿＿＿＿＿＿＿＿＿＿＿＿＿＿＿＿＿＿＿＿

＿＿＿＿＿＿＿＿＿＿＿＿＿＿＿＿＿＿＿＿＿

b. ＿＿＿＿＿＿＿＿＿＿＿＿＿＿＿＿＿＿＿＿

＿＿＿＿＿＿＿＿＿＿＿＿＿＿＿＿＿＿＿＿＿

＿＿＿＿＿＿＿＿＿＿＿＿＿＿＿＿＿＿＿＿＿

c. _____

_____

_____

d. _____

_____

_____

e. _____

_____

_____

1.20 Circle the *observable behavior,* written as an action verb phrase.

1.21 Draw a line under the *conditions.*

1.22 Draw a wavy line under the *standard or criterion.* If necessary, rewrite your objectives on a separate page.

You have now completed the first activity and have written a set of instructional objectives that relate to a challenging, interesting, and relevant educational goal. In the next activity, you will take one of these objectives and break it down into its component tasks.

1.23 Write any comments or constructive suggestions you have about this activity.

_____

_____

_____

_____

SUPPLEMENTARY EXERCISES

These supplementary exercises are to be used at your discretion and at the discretion of your instructor. They are designed to enrich the field activities by providing you with additional experiences. Their specific purpose is given at the beginning of each exercise.

Please arrange all school and institutional observations and interviews with your instructor before entering any facility. Each time the student participates in an observation or an interview, the following information should be provided with the report: the student's name; the location of the facility; the population served—including such items as the grade level and approximate ages of the students; the time of day; the day of the week; and the name of the supervisor who authorized the particular visit.

You should complete each exercise on a separate sheet of paper. Identify the exercise you are doing by its number and page in the book. At the end of each report, include your objective and subjective reactions to the exercise as well as suggestions for improving the experience.

1. School Observation: Goals and Objectives

Purpose: To familiarize you with educational goals and instructional objectives currently being pursued in instructional or institutional settings.

Arrange with your instructor to visit a school or an institution. Arrange ahead of time to conduct your observation during a period devoted to formal instruction or formal learning experiences. Please remember that visitors can disrupt the programs of schools and institutions; please sit quietly and unobtrusively and do not interrupt the students during formal instruction periods.

Observe the situation for approximately twenty minutes to an hour.

1. During this period of time, note the following:

a. the activities in which students were engaged

b. the materials used to supplement instruction

c. any purpose, goals, or objectives that were communicated to the student—orally by the teacher, in writing on the chalkboard, in handouts, or in the instructional material.

2. If the educational goals or instructional objectives were not clearly identifiable, try to guess what they were.

3. On the basis of this information, prepare a minimum of three formal instructional objectives based on what you've observed or inferred.

4. Arrange a meeting with the teacher or supervisor, during which you check on the appropriateness of the instructional objectives you've written. Refine or alter them if the interview reveals you should do so.

5. Comment briefly on the value the experience had for you and give any suggestions for improving this experience.

6. Drop a note to the persons in charge of the program you visited, thanking them for their hospitality and communicating what you learned from the experience.

2. Teacher Interview

Purpose: To acquaint you with some of the educational goals and instructional objectives towards which education is directed.

1. Remember to provide all the necessary preliminary information for observations and interviews described in the first supplementary exercise.

2. With the assistance of your instructor (if necessary), arrange a meeting with a teacher or institutional trainer or therapist, or with any other professional whose primary activity involves teaching, training, or counseling. When you make the appointment for the interview, ask the individual to bring along lesson plans, curriculum guides, and other materials related to the content of the instructional activities.

3. During a half-hour interview, informally discuss some of the general and specific educational goals the teacher's system, school, or institution is trying to help students or clients achieve. Then try to focus on one general educational goal and derive, with the teacher, some illustrative instructional objectives. (Many teachers do not conceptualize their goals as formal instructional objectives, so you should attempt to make this translation and check the appropriateness of your specification of the objectives with the teacher.)

4. After the interview, evaluate some of the teacher's educational goals and objectives in terms of student interest, challenge, and the other qualities listed in the first activity.

5. Include your own comments, impressions, and suggestions for improving the experience.

6. Drop a note to the people in charge of the program you visited, thanking them for their hospitality and communicating what you learned from the experience.

3. Library Research

Purpose: To familiarize you with sample educational goals and instructional objectives currently in operation in schools.

1. Go to a university library or to the library of the school-board office in your home area. Ask to see copies of school educational goals or instructional objectives. There will probably be some printed curriculum guides for the local or state school system. Write down the reference: author, title, publisher, date, pages.

2. Scan the material and try to identify at least *three to five* broad educational goals. Then determine whether these are stated as formal instructional objectives, including student responses and conditions and standards of performance.

3. Note at least three of these objectives. If objectives are not formally stated, try to take some of the material that you're reading and translate it into a set of formal instructional objectives.

4. Next, look at these objectives and comment upon their interest and their potential as challenging objectives. Add your own comments and suggestions.

4. Interview with Community Educational Representatives

Purpose: To familiarize you with the educational goals and objectives held by an individual who plays an active role in setting educational policy.

1. Make an appointment with a member of the local school board or committee. During the interview, try to find out this individual's perception of the goals of education in the school district.

2. Then ask the individual to offer some very specific objectives. If these are

not stated as formal instructional objectives, translate them—including student responses, conditions, and standards of performance. Ask the interviewee whether these are reasonable translations.

3. After the interview, comment upon the quality of the objectives in terms of their interest and challenge.

4. Add your own comments and suggestions.

SUGGESTED READINGS AND REFERENCES

Anderson, R. C., and Faust, G. W. *Educational Psychology: The Science of Instruction and Learning.* New York: Dodd, Mead & Co., 1973. Chapter 1, pp. 13–55 (instructional objectives).

Bushell, D., Jr. *Classroom Behavior.* Englewood Cliffs, N.J.: Prentice-Hall, 1974. Chapter 3, pp. 35–36 (instructional objectives).

DeCecco, J. P., and Crawford, W. R. *The Psychology of Learning and Instruction.* Englewood Cliffs, N.J.: Prentice-Hall, 1974. Chapter 2, pp. 24–35 (instructional objectives).

Gage, N. L., and Berliner, D. C. *Educational Psychology.* Chicago: Rand McNally College Publishing Co., 1975. Unit 3, pp. 37–47 (why and how to formulate instructional objectives).

Gagné, R. M. *Essentials of Learning for Instruction.* Hinsdale, Ill.: The Dryden Press, 1974. Chapter 4, pp. 72–77 (learning objectives and the stating of learning objectives).

Hamachek, D. E. *Behavior Dynamics in Teaching, Learning, and Growth.* Boston: Allyn & Bacon, 1975. Chapter 13, pp. 590–91 (the value of instructional objectives: pros and cons).

Lefrancois, G. R. *Psychology for Teaching.* Belmont, Ca.: Wadsworth Publishing Co., 1975. Chapter 6, pp. 112–14 (instructional objectives).

Mager, R. F. *Goal Analysis.* Belmont, Ca.: Fearon Publishers, 1972.

————, *Preparing Instructional Objectives.* Belmont, Ca.: Fearon Publishers, 1961.

Plowman, P. D. *Behavioral Objectives.* Chicago: Science Research Associates, 1971. Introduction, pp. xxii–xxviii (instructional objectives and educational goals).

Sulzer-Azaroff, B., and Mayer, G. R. *Applying Behavior Analysis Procedures with Children and Youth.* New York: Holt, Rinehart & Winston, 1977. Units 3, 4 (goals and objectives).

Sulzer, B., and Mayer, G. R. *Behavior Modification Procedures for School Personnel.* Hinsdale, Ill.: The Dryden Press, 1972. Chapter 1, pp. 4–8 (specifying behavioral goals and criterion level).

Taber, J. I.; Glaser, R.; and Schaefer, H. H. *Learning and Programmed Instruction.* Reading, Mass.: Addison-Wesley Publishing Co., 1965. Chapter 1, pp. 3–5, pp. 62–65 (instructional objectives).

Vargas, J. S. *Writing Worthwhile Behavioral Objectives.* New York: Harper & Row, 1972.

2
ANALYZING COMPONENT SUBTASKS

Objectives

Assuming that you have already mastered some textual materials on learning taxonomies and the analysis of instructional tasks, on completing this activity you should be able to:

- Define a *task analysis* and discuss its function.

- Break down instructional tasks into subtasks.

- Rough out a task analysis—in outline and flow-diagram form.

- Select subtasks in varied functional modes—cognitive, psychomotor, and affective (if appropriate).

- Select relevant and sophisticated subtasks by identifying, labeling, defining, and illustrating the six levels of cognition and including some subtasks from the higher levels of cognition in a task analysis.

- Complete a task analysis in final form, including the crucial subtasks of a student-selected instructional objective.

Analyzing Component Tasks

In this activity you are asked to choose one of your instructional objectives and write a complete *task analysis* for it. A task analysis describes in detail the actions required for the student to demonstrate attainment of the objective. Describe the actions in terms of their function or of the results that the performance will produce. In a task analysis you do not necessarily need to describe *how* the student will add two three-digit numbers together mentally (whether by "counting them up" or memorizing the combinations), but you do need to indicate that the student will have to be able to add single columns of numbers, to "carry" the tens digit to the next column left, to proceed through the columns in the proper order, and to place the final "carried" digit in the far left column of the sum. A complete task analysis will indicate all the necessary behaviors from demonstrating attainment of the instructional objective back to the point at which the student begins the instructional sequence. Deciding where these "beginning points" are will be part of your experience in the next activity. Here you'll simply analyze the behaviors as completely as possible without reducing them to absurdity by including behaviors so elementary that your students don't need to learn them.

To perform a task analysis, the observable act in an instructional objective is broken down into its component behavioral subtasks. These less complex preparatory behaviors are often referred to as *en-route behaviors*. *Enabling objectives* are objectives that contain en-route behaviors, stated with their appropriate conditions and standards of acceptability. The ability to perform all of these subtasks or en-route behaviors *enables* the student to learn to perform the behaviors designated in the instructional objective.

Preparing a Task Analysis

Here is a partial task analysis.

Educational goal: The student should learn to swim.

One of the many possible *instructional objectives:* The student should be able to swim four lengths of the pool without stopping, using an acceptable crawl stroke. ("Acceptable" means that the student's breathing and arm and leg strokes are as described in Red Cross instruction books.)

Enabling objectives—The student should be able to:

1. demonstrate a proper flutter kick
   Subtasks: in conjunction with face float; using kick board by kicking as described in text for one length of the pool; kicking while holding on to the side of the pool; kicking on mat.
2. demonstrate correct breathing technique
   Subtasks: in conjunction with arm movements; while holding the side of the pool; while lying on a mat.
3. demonstrate correct arm motion
   Subtasks: in conjunction with breathing; while floating on the face; while standing, with the face in the water.
4. describe either orally or in writing the proper kicking, breathing, and arm movements as described in the text.
5. observe demonstrations by the instructor and by other students and discriminate acceptable from nonacceptable kicking, breathing, and leg movements.
6. do a face float for 20 seconds.
7. put the face in the water for 20 seconds.
8. enter the water and get wet, and so on.

Sometimes a task analysis is better expressed as a flow diagram. In figure 2 you can see a visual presentation of the preceding task analysis, demonstrating the logical ordering of subtasks. Each subtask enables the accomplishment of the next. We have probably detailed the breathing aspect of the crawl stroke more than necessary, since most students can enter the

Figure 2 *Flow diagram of a task analysis.*

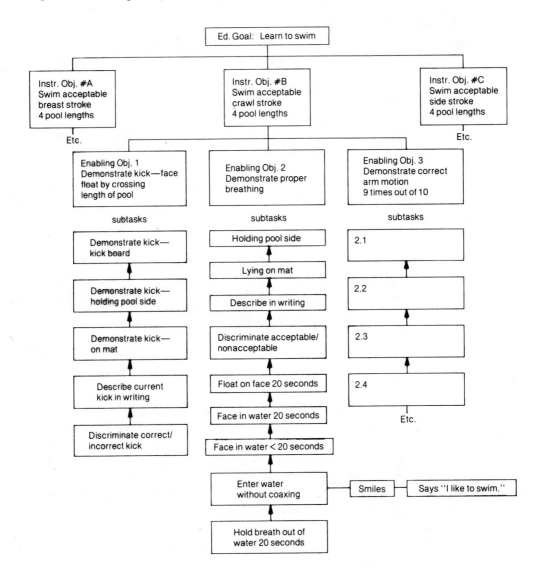

water and hold their breath on land. However, if you were working with students with inordinate fears or physical problems, such specification might be necessary.

2.1, 2.2, 2.3   In figure 2, four boxes in the flow diagram have been left blank. You should fill in 2.1, 2.2, and 2.3 by referring to the third enabling objective ("demonstrate correct arm motion") in the written task analysis.

2.4   Carry the task analysis one step further by composing the contents of box 2.4 by yourself.

If the educational goal were fully developed into all its component instructional objectives, you can see a more thorough curriculum would result. Similarly, when an instructor takes an instructional objective and analyzes it into all its enabling objectives and subtasks, the ensuing instruction will be more thorough.

2.5   Take a sheet of paper and begin to rough out an outline for a task analysis. (Label the sheet 2.5.) Do this by selecting one of the instructional objectives that you formulated for Activity 1. Be sure your instructional objective appears at the top of the analysis and that subtasks include a student-performed action verb.

2.6   Now rough out a flow diagram on a second sheet to show the order and interrelation of the tasks. (Label the sheet 2.6.)

Including Varied Subtasks

The components of an instructional objective often are varied modes of behavior. A complete task analysis usually identifies not only knowledge but also actions, feelings, and attitudes. Therefore a complete task analysis includes not only the cognitive (intellectual or knowledge) function, but also, when appropriate, the psychomotor (physical) and affective (emotional) functions as well. Our swimming task analysis in figure 2 includes primarily psychomotor subtasks (kicking, holding, floating). However, you'll notice some cognitive tasks (discriminate, describe in writing), and some affective "subtasks" that reflect how the student "feels" about the activity (smiles, says, "I like swimming"). Some subtasks may combine more than one mode (enters water—psychomotor; without coaxing—affective).

2.7   Here is a list of some other subtasks. To help you to recognize varied response modes, indicate whether each subtask is *primarily* cognitive (C), psychomotor (P), or affective (A).

   a. Uses tools correctly to obtain an intact specimen. _____

   b. Identifies each of five different ferns. _____

   c. Conceptualizes a theory of the evolution of a given rock formation on the basis of fern fossils. _____

   d. Registers for all the available courses on the topic, reads about it during spare time, and spends free time hunting for specimens for a collection. _____

   e. Prepares a slide for microscopic examination by slicing the specimen into thin sections. _____

   f. Describes how to use tools correctly to obtain an intact specimen. _____

   g. Skips into classroom with a smile. _____

2.8   Refer to the task-analysis outline you roughed out for 2.5. In the margin, label each task as cognitive (C), psychomotor (P), or affective (A). For example:

Floats on face   P

2.9   Have you included varied modes of behavior in your task analysis? Yes _____ No _____
Try to add some subtasks from each category (C, P, A), if this appears reasonable.

Striving for Relevance and Sophistication in the Selection of Cognitive Subtasks

Cognitive subtasks often constitute a major portion of formal instruction. Even when the instructional objective is primarily psychomotor (as with our example based on swimming), some cognitive aspects are usually included in instruction to enhance learning. These may be in the form of descriptions used for classification. For example, for the subtask "discriminates correct kick"—what are the critical features of a proper kick? They may include a specification of the angle of the knee bend.

Unfortunately, it seems that those cognitive tasks easiest to specify are not necessarily the most relevant or sophisticated. Perhaps this is why some social-studies teachers are addicted to teaching names or dates. To assist you in avoiding such pitfalls in your own instructional planning, we shall review with you an adaptation of one of the standard analyses of the levels of cognitive behavior.* This system includes two broad categories—knowledge and intellectual skills (comprehension, application, analysis, synthesis, and evaluation).

Knowledge (know) is the lowest level of cognition. It involves memorization and the recall of specific facts or systems. Defining terms ("Botany is . . ."); recalling features ("There is a cellular wall . . ."); stating rules or conventions of form ("A paragraph is indented five spaces . . ."); relating events in time ("The warming of the glaciers was followed by a period of . . ."); recalling classification schemes or criteria of theories or of relationships ("As the earth moves nearer to the sun in its orbit . . ."); "Darwin claimed that a system of natural selection created . . ."); and recalling principles and generalizations are all knowledge-related activities.

Intellectual skills include:

- *Comprehension (comp)*, what we frequently refer to as "understanding" when we attempt to define cognitive behavior. It requires that the individual make use of the material in some way other than simply repeating it, but without necessarily grasping its implications or relating it to any other information. Translation (arithmetic word problems), summarization (writing a précis of an article), or interpretation (giving new examples or rewordings) are examples of comprehension performances.

- *Application (app)* of abstractions to particular concrete situations. The use of principles, generalized methods, rules, or theories is included in this category. The recording system you will create for Activity 4 requires application of the principles defined within the unit.

*This analysis of the levels of cognitive behavior is adapted from B. S. Bloom, *Taxonomy of Educational Objectives, Handbook I* (New York: Longmans, Green, 1956).

- *Analysis (ana)*, the selection of particular elements from a whole. The task analysis is the best example. Clarification of the whole often involves analysis of its components. Recognition of unstated assumptions, relating data to hypotheses, discovering systematic arrangements, or picking out patterns underlying artistic or literary works are all forms of analysis.

- *Synthesis (synth)*, the reverse of analysis. Instead of breaking down the whole into its components, several separate elements must be brought together to form a cohesive unit. Instead of discovering a structure or an arrangement, the individual creates a new one. Production of plans (for example, designing a lesson), most sophisticated forms of communication (writing a speech), formulation of theories from facts, and making modifications according to data are all behaviors classified as synthesis.

- *Evaluation (eval)*, a judgment activity. This requires the comparing of materials to criteria, decisions about the usefulness of certain methods for particular purposes, or comparisons of different interpretations or generalizations.

You'll notice that these cognitive behaviors start at the simplest level and work towards the most complex and sophisticated. Each level is usually supported by a base of lower-level cognitive behaviors. For example, to apply rules *(app)*, the rules must first have been acquired *(comp)*. To design something by combining elements *(synth)*, the student must first be familiar with the function of the elements *(comp)*. Therefore, it is likely that a task analysis will include cognitive behaviors at several levels.

2.10 To give you some practice in analyzing cognitive subtasks, label each of the following *know, comp, app, ana, synth,* or *eval.* (If more than one level is involved, select the highest level.)

  a. When shown a quarter, nickel, and three pennies, says "thirty-three cents." _____

  b. Composes a short musical selection in the Baroque style. _____

  c. Wires a circuit from a diagram. _____

d. Develops a theory about the impact of industrialization upon public education. _____

e. Awards a blue ribbon to the most skillfully crafted piece of furniture. _____

f. Explains the use of dining utensils. _____

g. Takes an instructional objective and dissects it into its behavioral components. _____

2.11 Now you should be prepared to classify the levels of the cognitive subtasks in your task analysis. List each cognitive subtask below and label its *cognitive level*.

Cognitive Subtask	Cognitive Level
_____	_____
_____	_____
_____	_____
_____	_____
_____	_____
_____	_____
_____	_____
_____	_____
_____	_____

If you have fewer than ten, leave the extra spaces empty; if you have more than ten, write the additional items on a separate sheet of paper.

2.12   Refer to 2.11 and evaluate the levels of cognitive behavior included in your task analysis.

a.   Are several levels included? _____

b.   Are some higher-level subtasks included? _____

c.   If you answered *no* to 2.12a or 2.12b, try to design a few more cognitive subtasks so your task analysis contains both varied levels of cognitive behavior and higher-level subtasks. Write them here.

Cognitive Subtasks   Cognitive Level

_____   _____

_____   _____

_____   _____

_____   _____

_____   _____

_____   _____

_____   _____

_____   _____

2.13   The next page is blank. Fill it with your task analysis in its final form—either as a written sequence or as a flow diagram. While the number of subtasks will vary depending on your instructional objective, you should aim for ten to twenty subtasks.

2.13   Task analysis.

Educational Goal: _____

Instructional Objective: _____

Task Analysis (enabling objectives and subtasks):

_____

Because this unit is so important, and because you will be building upon this work, review your work in Activities 1 and 2 before going on to the next activity. If you answer *no* to any of the questions listed in 2.14, go back *now* and make the necessary revisions. Remember that tasks and objectives are rarely written perfectly the first time. Revision is not a sign of failure, but an indication that you have viewed your material more thoroughly or from a better perspective. Do not be afraid to rewrite or regroup your original ideas.

Use your refined instructional objective and task analysis to complete the rest of the activities, if possible. However, feel free to substitute another instructional objective and other subtasks if, after restating them, your original objective and subtasks prove unworkable in later activities. Remember, though, that you have already invested much time and effort in selecting your present objective and subtasks and that they are probably very well formulated. So if they seem inappropriate later, consider a careful rewording before you eliminate them completely. Now for your final checkover.

2.14 a. Are your instructional objective, enabling objectives, and subtasks written as observable student behaviors? _____

   b. Are your instructional objective and enabling objectives written in complete sentences with action verbs? _____

   c. Do your instructional objective, enabling objectives, and subtasks indicate behaviors necessary to the performance of the educational goal as it is stated? _____

   d. Have you missed including any crucial subtasks in your task analysis? _____

   e. Have you included the various forms (cognitive, affective, psychomotor) of behavior that are relevant to your instructional objective? _____

   f. Do any cognitive tasks you analyzed include most of the levels of cognitive behavior? _____

2.15   Write any comments or constructive suggestions you have about this activity.

_____

_____

_____

_____

You now have a well-specified set of tasks upon which to build the rest of your instructional plan. The beginning is _more_ than half the battle!

SUPPLEMENTARY EXERCISES

(For general instructions, see the Supplementary Exercises for Activity 1.)

1. School Observation to Construct a Task Analysis

Purpose: To acquaint you with some sample educational tasks designed to achieve specific goals or objectives.

1. Arrange with your instructor to visit a school. Try to attend a session of between one-half hour and an hour, during a time in which formal instruction is scheduled.

2. Describe in detail the activities in which the students are engaging. Include their _responses_, the _conditions_ under which they are responding, and any _evaluation_ that is going on. Also indicate if the goals of the activity have been communicated to the student, and in what manner.

3. Arrange with the teacher to meet at a time of mutual convenience to discuss the purpose of the activities, particularly how they relate to a broader set of goals. During that conversation, ask how the activity fits into a general sequence of instructional tasks and see if you can construct a portion of the task analysis, indicating the activity you have observed and its relation to other subtasks.

4. Following the interview, comment upon the logic and any other aspects of the subtask sequence that you feel are important. Look at the subtasks in the task analysis and evaluate the variety of modes of student activities they offer. Are there psychomotor, affective, and cognitive objectives?

5. Include your own comments and suggestions.

2. Library Research on Task Analyses

Purpose: To familiarize you with sample instructional activities and tasks.

1. Go to a local curriculum library at a university, school board, or committee office. Ask to see curriculum guides for the local or state school systems.

2. Look at some of the suggested instructional activities. Try to construct a portion of a task analysis that incorporates a series of activities.

3. Judge whether the series of subtasks leads in a logical fashion to the acquisition of the objectives.

4. Look at the subtasks in the task analysis and evaluate the variety of modes of student activities they offer—are there psychomotor, affective, and cognitive activities? If there are cognitive objectives, what level of cognition do they represent?

5. Include your own comments and suggestions.

SUGGESTED READINGS AND REFERENCES

Anderson, R. C., and Faust, G. W. *Educational Psychology: The Science of Instruction and Learning.* New York: Dodd, Mead & Co., 1973. Chapter 2, pp. 57–84 (task analysis).

Biehler, R. F. *Psychology Applied to Teaching.* Boston: Houghton Mifflin Co., 1971. Chapter 8, pp. 281–82 (task analysis).

Bloom, B. S. *Taxonomy of Educational Objectives.* New York: David McKay Co., 1956.

DeCecco, J. P., and Crawford, W. R. *The Psychology of Learning and Instruction.* Englewood Cliffs, N.J.: Prentice-Hall, 1974. Chapter 2, pp. 35–37 (task analysis).

Klausmeier, H. J., and Goodwin, W. *Learning and Human Abilities: Educational Psychology.* 4th

ed. New York: Harper & Row, Publishers, 1966. Chapter 4, p. 98 (analysis of objectives).

Mager, R. F. *Goal Analysis.* Belmont, Ca.: Fearon Publishers, 1972. Pp. 1–132 (goal analysis).

Plowman, P. D. *Behavioral Objectives.* Chicago: Science Research Associates, 1971. Chapter 9, pp. 179–88 (cognitive skills).

Smith, M. D. *Educational Psychology and Its Classroom Applications.* Boston: Allyn & Bacon, 1975. Chapter 15, pp. 429–33 (task analysis and three domains of skills).

Taber, J. I.; Glaser, R.; and Schaefer, H. H. *Learning and Programmed Instruction.* Reading, Mass.: Addison-Wesley, 1965. Chapter 4, pp. 73–83 (task taxonomies or analysis).

3

ENTERING BEHAVIORS AND OTHER PREREQUISITE BEHAVIORS

Objectives

Assuming that you have mastered textual material on human development—such as Piaget's theory of cognitive development and theories of social learning and behavior analysis—and have familiarized yourself with the developmental and cultural characteristics of the students you expect to teach, on completing this activity you should be able to:

- Specify the relevant entering behaviors for the instruction you plan to design.

- Describe any characteristics of your students that may affect entering behavior.

- Describe and use instructional adaptations—in the form of modified objectives or procedural descriptions—to correct for differences between your students' actual and expected or desired entering behaviors.

- Design effective procedures for dealing with special situations that may arise in group instruction because of the individual differences among students.

Entering Behaviors and Other Prerequisite Behaviors

Formal learning usually involves building a set of skills or performances upon others; the ability to perform several simple tasks may be necessary before it is possible to learn a complex task. You have already seen this as you constructed your task analysis and discovered the many subtasks necessary to achieve the single instructional objective you selected. You have a general idea of the ordering of subtasks necessary to achieve the instructional objective. Now you must decide where in that sequence your instruction will begin.

Adapting Instruction to Entering Behaviors

It is of crucial importance to find the appropriate subtasks with which to initiate instruction. Instructing students to perform behaviors already well established in their repertoires wastes your time and theirs—but problems *will* arise if you assume that the students have particular *entering behaviors* that they actually do not possess. They will be confused and discouraged when they fail in their attempt to do something for which they are not properly prepared. This activity is designed to help you assess the abilities your students possess before you begin instruction—their *entering behaviors.*

Know your students. As you are working through this activity, you should be realistic about the students you are likely to be teaching when you actually use the instruction you develop. If, for instance, you are teaching reading to second-grade children in a college town, you might reasonably expect them to speak some close approximation of standard English—or at least to be familiar enough with the way it sounds to be able to discriminate between grammatical and ungrammatical language while reading aloud. If you will be teaching inner-city children, however, you cannot assume that their spoken language will be in the standard grammatical form. Indeed, it is entirely possible that language very different from what you consider standard English will sound perfectly grammatical to them, and that "book English" will sound foreign. Most people find that their own manner of speaking sounds correct and that any other feels awkward. The child who is unfamiliar with the language used in texts may be seriously hampered in the attempt to learn reading skills, and may require special adaptive teaching procedures.

Suppose you are teaching cursive writing. One entering behavior you might consider is the student's ability to hold a pencil properly. This may seem an uncomplicated subskill that all children can perform. You could usually assume that your students possess this entering behavior. However, remember that retarded or very young children (or even those with inadequate or inappropriate training) may not possess such simple physical skills. Perhaps the problem that produced a child's retardation has affected other aspects of performance. Many mentally retarded children have other organic or developmental difficulties that result in such problems as spastic muscles or incongruous movement patterns. The set of entering behaviors you can expect from retarded or very young children does not necessarily include the fine motor coordination you can expect from the average second-grade child. Chronological age, grade placement, even mental age—none of these is a sure indication of the presence or absence of a given behavior. This is why it is so important for teachers to know the capabilities and deficiencies of their individual students.

Identifying Essential Entering Behaviors for
Learning Given Subtasks

This section is designed to help you identify and describe those particular entering behaviors necessary for the subtasks you are considering teaching. Remember that the entering behaviors you identify should be abilities that are essential foundations for the new behaviors you plan to teach. You are describing the relevant abilities of your students before the beginning of instruction. In the next section you will describe your students and then return to this list of entering behaviors to decide whether they are likely to be part of your students' behavioral repertoires. In Activity 6 you will return to this list and design a procedure for assessing exactly which of these behaviors your students actually possess. You will be able to use this pre-assessment before presenting your instruction.

You have already selected an instructional objective and analyzed its component enabling objectives and subtasks. Here you will be asked to refer to Activity 2.13 and to select two enabling objectives for which you will design instruction. Now look at each of those enabling objectives and locate its constituent subtasks—those that serve as its foundation. (For example, "face in water for 20 seconds" is an entering behavior for "float on face for 20 seconds.") The lower-level subtasks are the *entering behaviors* essential to the acquisition of new behaviors. (Activity 3.8 will ask you to return to Activities 3.2–3.4 to indicate the likelihood that these entering behaviors will be present in the students' behavioral repertoires—do nothing with the columns on the right at this time.)

Instructional objective _____

_____

3.1 Enabling objective # _____ (Select a component enabling objective of the instructional objective for which you would like to design instruction.) If an enabling objective is too complex or time consuming for your students, select a subtask of the enabling objective as the

basis for designing your instruction. _____

_____

3.2 Essential entering behaviors (complete only those that are applicable to your enabling objective or subtask—if not applicable, write *N.A.*).

		Present	Not Present
a. Psychomotor behaviors ("hold a pencil,"			
"draw a circle"): _____		_____	_____
_____		_____	_____
_____		_____	_____

  Not

b. Cognitive behaviors: Present Present

Knowledge _____ _____ _____

_____ _____ _____

Comprehension _____ _____ _____

_____ _____ _____

Application _____ _____ _____

_____ _____ _____

Analysis _____ _____ _____

_____ _____ _____

Synthesis _____ _____ _____

_____ _____ _____

Evaluation _____ _____ _____

_____ _____ _____

c. Affective behaviors ("chooses writing activity when given a choice of various activities"): _____ _____ _____

_____ _____ _____

3.3   Enabling objective # ____ (Select another enabling objective or subtask for which you would like to design an instructional sequence.)

_____

_____

3.4   Essential entering behaviors (complete only those that are applicable to your task—if not applicable, write *N.A.*).

		Present	Not Present
a.	Psychomotor behaviors: _____	_____	_____
	_____	_____	_____
b.	Cognitive behaviors:		
	Knowledge _____	_____	_____
	Comprehension _____	_____	_____
	Application _____	_____	_____
	Analysis _____	_____	_____
	Synthesis _____	_____	_____
	Evaluation _____	_____	_____
c.	Affective behaviors: _____	_____	_____
	_____	_____	_____
	_____	_____	_____

Other Behaviors That May Facilitate or Impede Learning

Activities 3.1–3.4 were essentially a review of the components of a given instructional objective. Besides entering behaviors directly related to sub-tasks, some individual behaviors may also be prerequisites for attaining the behavior specified in the instructional objectives. Among these may be *communication skills* (reading, writing, speaking); *social skills* (the ability to work despite frustrations, to follow directions, to work cooperatively in a group); and other *learning facilitation skills* (sticking with a task to completion, working in the absence of extrinsic rewards, or working under delayed-reward conditions.

3.5   List the communication, emotional, social, and learning-facilitation skills essential to the first enabling objective you listed (3.1).

_____

_____

3.6   To the second (3.3). _____

_____

Focusing on Your Students

The previous section focused on the enabling objectives (or subtasks) you hope to teach and the entering behaviors requisite to teaching them successfully. Here the focus shifts to the students themselves. Developing a description of your students will provide you with a clearer perspective on the appropriateness of the tasks you've written and of the entering behaviors these tasks require.

3.7   Write a brief description of your students. Feel free to adapt this form to your own situation—the "student" may be a "patient," "trainee," or "counselee." (Try to locate an actual student. If you do not have any students and your instructor has been unable to make appropriate arrangements for you, you may describe a hypothetical case. If your description is hypothetical, check yes.) Yes. _____

a.   Number of students   _____

b.   Age and sex   _____ Grade level _____

c.   Physical development (maturation) and general physical characteristics (what kinds of gross and fine motor abilities are they likely to possess—for example, can they sit comfortably on the floor?)

_____

_____

_____

d. Social and emotional development and learning-facilitation skills

_____

_____

e. Probable verbal abilities and types of verbal interaction with which

they are likely to have had experience _____

_____

_____

f. Cognitive abilities (described in terms of Piaget's theory of development, or any other developmental taxonomy with which you are familiar—see suggested readings for sources).

_____

_____

_____

g. Previous school experience (public or private, standard classroom or progressive, general curriculum or specialized)

_____

_____

Now you have described your students' various characteristics. Previously you described the skills your students should possess as entering behaviors before you could begin instruction for the selected enabling objectives or subtasks. The next step is pretty obvious—are the abilities of your students and the required entering behaviors likely to agree?

3.8 From your class description, decide whether or not your students are likely to possess the entering behaviors you listed as relevant to the enabling objectives or subtasks you selected (3.2, 3.4). Check "present" or "not present" to the right of each behavior you listed and be prepared to explain your answer.

Name: _____

3.9   You have covered a lot of ground and made several major decisions. To be certain you're on the right track, please complete this sheet, tear it out, and have it approved by your instructor before beginning Activity 4.

Class description (three or four sentences summarizing the factors you consider important):

_____

_____

_____

_____

_____

_____

Instructional objective: _____

_____

_____

_____

Major entering behaviors for enabling objective (or subtask) #1:

_____

_____

_____

Enabling objective (or subtask) #1: _____

_____

Major entering behaviors for enabling objective (or subtask) #2:

_____

_____

_____

Enabling objective (or subtask) #2: _____

_____

Other prerequisite behaviors: _____

_____

Estimated time required to teach enabling objective (or subtask) #1:

_____

Estimated time required to teach enabling objective (or subtask) #2:

_____

Comments: _____

_____

_____

_____

DO NOT WRITE BELOW THIS LINE

OK to go ahead _____

NOTE TO INSTRUCTOR: Instructors wishing to maintain quality control should check tasks for the criteria listed in Activity 1 *(challenging, interesting,* and *relevant).*

Adjusting for Disparities between Requisite Entering Behaviors and Student Behavioral Repertoires

The more knowledgeable you are about children's development—including knowledge of such subjects as behavior analysis, social learning and development, Piagetian stages of cognitive development, and anthropological factors and development—the better equipped you are to match instructional tasks to individual students. However, educated guesses will not always be correct, since every student is unique. Equipped with different physical characteristics that limit or facilitate development, each student experiences different learning episodes.

Each *group* of students is also unique. One of the joys of teaching is the variety of students with whom you become acquainted and the accompanying classroom styles you can develop for dealing most effectively with each group. If you are to adapt your instruction to each group or student effectively, you need some specific plans for altering your original objective and instructional sequence, or you need methods to overcome deficiencies in student behaviors so they eventually meet the entering behaviors required for successful instruction.

Assess Prerequisite Behaviors

The most appropriate method for determining whether students actually possess necessary entering behaviors and other prerequisite behaviors is to objectively check them. In the activity on *evaluation* (Activity 6), you will be asked to design an instrument to conduct such a formal assessment of prerequisite behaviors. At this point you should think about the most appropriate method for accomplishing this. If the entering behavior is "puts face in water," the method of assessment might be "ask student to put face in water and check yes or no." To determine whether a student can remain on a task for a given period of time, assign several sample tasks and see how long it takes the student to complete them. If algebra skills are necessary prerequisites for a college physics course, test students on sample algebra problems. (If you feel unclear about how to select appropriate assessment procedures, turn to Activity 6 and skim through the material between 6.1 and 6.2.)

3.10   For enabling objective (or subtask) #1, briefly describe how you might assess prerequisite behaviors.

_____

_____

3.11   Do the same for enabling objective (or subtask) #2.

_____

_____

Adjust to Disparities

Although you will actually conduct this assessment in the future, you should begin now to develop a method for adjusting disparities between prerequisite behaviors and the actual repertoires of your students. There are several things you can do to remedy such disparities. Choose one of the alternatives listed below and describe the changes in your lesson plan that would be necessary to accommodate your students' having *too few* of the required entering behaviors. If you feel some combination of these techniques would be most appropriate, employ more than one. Describe the changes that each alternative requires separately. Keep clear in your mind why you are making each change and why the alternatives you have chosen are appropriate.

A. Increase entering behaviors through review exercises.

B. Provide more instruction than you had previously intended.

C. Change your instructional objectives by lowering the standards of performance.

3.12   I would choose alternative(s) A   B   C   (circle one or more), and therefore would (describe the changes you would make—specific review exercises, content of additional instruction, exact criteria changes, and time allotment):

_____

_____

_____

3.13   List two new or revised enabling objectives or subtasks that would be appropriate for more *advanced entering behaviors* than anticipated. It is quite likely that in your original task analysis you broke down the component skills of your instructional objective into initial skills that have already been well-established in your students' repertoires.

a. Original enabling objective or subtask _____

_____

Revised enabling objective or subtask _____

_____

b. Original enabling objective or subtask _____

_____

Revised enabling objective or subtask _____

_____

Individual Differences and Group Instruction

As you continue in your study of educational psychology and other areas of education, you will learn various methods for individualizing instruction—methods that provide for differences in your students' behavioral repertoires and learning abilities. The more closely individual students' abilities are reflected in the instruction they receive, the more successfully they will learn. The most exciting classrooms today are those in which each student is occupied with his or her own task—one that is challenging, yet in which the student is very likely to succeed. There are some instructional activities, however, that are most appropriate for groups of students: for example, choral singing, games, committee work, and group experiments.

Here we'd like you to describe a couple of situations arising from individual differences in instruction-related behaviors during a group-instruction episode. (Please do not discuss management or discipline problems here; we will deal with them in a later activity.) Try to choose a problem you are likely to encounter. If you have any trouble describing or inventing situations, think back to the good old days and try to recall some classroom scene that involved an unusual or memorable student, maybe even a notorious one! You should have no trouble recalling several of those characters and the situations they created. Remember that girl who used to turn in her exam paper while you were still working on the first question? You probably had someone in one of your classes who usually failed to keep up with the rest of the class, even though you knew he worked harder than you did. What about the one who used to get confused every time a task involved long division?

3.14 Describe one situation. _____

_____

_____

_____

a. How would this situation affect accomplishment of the enabling objective or subtask you would be teaching? _____

_____

b. How would you deal with this situation? Indicate the specific procedures you would follow. _____

_____

_____

_____

c. Refer to your student description (3.7). Would the procedure you have chosen be effective with the students you described? How might the students described in the situation react? How might the other students in the class react? _____

_____

_____

3.15   Describe a second situation. _____

_____

_____

_____

a. How would it affect accomplishment of the enabling objectives or

subtasks you would be teaching? _____

_____

b. How would you deal with this situation? Indicate the specific proce-

dures you would follow. _____

_____

_____

_____

c. Refer to your student description (3.7). Would the procedure you
have chosen be effective with the students you described? How
might the students described in the situation react? How might the

other students in the class react? _____

_____

_____

Now you have planned in detail where you hope to go and where you
will start. You also know some adjustments that can be made to accommodate individual differences. The next activity will give you some guidelines for monitoring progress and avoiding or coping with management
problems.

You have accomplished a lot. Good for you!

MAKING EDUCATIONAL PSYCHOLOGY WORK

3.16   What comments or suggestions do you have? _____

_____

_____

_____

SUPPLEMENTARY EXERCISES

1. School Observation and Teacher Interview

Purpose: To provide you with the experience of determining how classroom activities can be adjusted to meet the behavioral repertoires of individual students.

1. Arrange with your instructor to visit a local school during a time for which formal instruction is scheduled. Observe the activities or tasks in which the students are engaging.

2. Schedule a meeting with the teacher at a time of mutual convenience.

3. Discuss with the teacher how entering behaviors were determined. Was it assumed that all students were ready to move into this next activity? Were students working at different levels and at different paces? Were any formal or informal assessment procedures used? Did the students demonstrate their completion or acquisition of subtasks directly subordinate to the current subtasks?

4. Ask the teacher if there were students who were responding differently from most of the other students—for example, was there a student who was far behind the other students? Who did not possess the entering behaviors? Who had an unusual interest in the material, or was particularly uninterested in it? Who was particularly gifted in the subject?

5. What adjustments have been made for such students?

6. Describe the developmental level of the students in the class—their motor development, how they seem to be able to handle large and small objects; their size and physical development; how mature they seem to be emotionally; and their apparent level of cognitive development. (You might refer to Piaget's classifications at this point, or to one of the other analyses of child development.)

7. Do the students behave in a manner appropriate to their developmental level?

8. Comment on the appropriateness of the selection of tasks for this group of students.

9. Include your own comments and suggestions.

2. Observing Students' Developmental Level

Purpose: To integrate your readings on human development and to focus your attention on developmental aspects of your students' behavior.

Read a source on child development, one that discusses the stages of physical, emotional, social, intellectual, and personal development, and then arrange with your instructor to visit some child- or youth-service facility, such as a school or day-care center. You should try to observe each of the following items:

1. Describe the physical size, activity level, eye-hand coordination, and other physical developmental characteristics of the students.

2. Estimate how long students appear to be able to persist at a task before tiring.

3. Describe the social interactions of the students. With whom are they relating during the formal program? With whom are they relating during unstructured times, such as free play or recess? Describe the nature of the social interactions.

4. Is any cognitive instruction going on? If so, describe it and try to relate it to what you know about children's cognitive performance at that developmental level.

5. Describe the apparent emotional level of the children. Do they seem to be able to work for long periods of time in the absence of any visible reward or reinforcement? How do the students react to frustration?

6. Describe the individual or personal development of a few of the children. Particularly note the use of unstructured time and apparent attitudes towards the self.

7. Write a summary statement comparing and contrasting what you observed about this group of students with what you have read in the literature on child development.

8. Include your own comments and suggestions.

3. Viewing Films on Human Development

Purpose: To provide you with an audio-visual experience on human development.

Arrange with your instructor to view one of the many films that have recently been produced on the various areas of child development. These include material on Piagetian development, language development, social behavior, and programs for preschool children.

1. List the title, producer, and distributor of the film. Also, if available, list the date of production.

2. Describe in one or two sentences the purpose of the film.

3. Outline the major points made in the film. For each major point, discuss or describe the illustrative material shown.

4. Comment on the value of the film to you as a student.

5. Compare what the film has described with what you have been reading about in your course material.

6. Include your own comments and suggestions.

4. Planning for Students with Special Needs

Purpose: To guide you in planning for students with special needs.

This exercise can be conducted through a teacher interview, a school observation, or the use of library materials.

1. Using one of the resources listed above, identify an instructional sequence—for example, a brief set of curriculum materials or a teacher's plan.

2. Briefly outline the sequence of steps in the instruction.

3. Describe any adjustments that would be made if the following problem situations presented themselves.

a. A student already had demonstrated mastery of the objectives for the lesson.

b. A student showed some unusual or very strong interest in the particular material.

c. A student did not possess the necessary entering behaviors to profit from the instruction.

d. A student had a physical impairment that interfered with his or her participation in the instructional sequence.

e. A student had a sensory (visual, oral, auditory) problem in working with the material.

5. Suggest some adjustments you would make in planning or carrying out the instruction for some of the students described above.

6. Include your own comments and suggestions.

5. Book or Chapter Report

Purpose: To enrich your knowledge of, and to provide a different perspective on, human development.

1. Select a book or a chapter on human development, preferably material relevant to the students you are now teaching or anticipate teaching.

2. List the author(s), title, publisher, date of publication, and page numbers of the book or chapter.

3. In one sentence, describe the main purpose of the book or chapter.

4. Outline the major topics covered in the material.

5. For each major topic, list the major points and give a few examples.

6. Relate the material you have read to the assigned material for your course by describing at least five similarities and five differences between this text and the text(s) assigned for the course.

7. Evaluate this material in light of your needs as a student and teacher; your reaction to the author's style, use of illustrations, and major points; and what you feel you have learned from reading this material.

8. Include your own comments and suggestions.

SUGGESTED READINGS AND REFERENCES

Anderson, R. C., and Faust, G. W. *Educational Psychology: The Science of Instruction and Learning.* New York: Dodd, Mead & Co., 1973. Chapter 3, pp. 85–124 (entering behavior).

Bandura, A. *Principles of Behavior Modification.* New York: Holt, Rinehart & Winston, 1969.

Bijou, S. W. "Development in the Pre-School Years: A Functional Analysis." *American Psychologist* 30 (1975): 829–37.

DeCecco, J. P., and Crawford, W. R. *The Psychology of Learning and Instruction.* Englewood Cliffs, N.J.: Prentice-Hall, 1974. Chapter 3, pp. 46–69 (entering behavior).

Gagné, R. M. "Learning Hierarchies." *Educational Psychologist* 6 (1968): 1–6. (A discussion of learning hierarchies and their development. This article presents a method for determining the entering behaviors students must have to learn a given lesson.)

Smith, M.D., *Educational Psychology and Its Classroom Applications.* Boston: Allyn & Bacon, 1975. Chapter 15, pp. 432–38 (entering behavior).

Taber, J. I.; Glaser, R.; and Schaefer, H. H. *Learning and Programmed Instruction.* Reading, Mass.: Addison-Wesley Publishing Co., 1965. Chapter 7, p. 147 (entering behavior); chapter 8, pp. 165–66 (assessment of entering behavior).

Wadsworth, B. J. *Piaget's Theory of Cognitive Development.* New York: David McKay Co., 1971.

4

RECORD KEEPING, FEEDBACK, AND AVOIDING AND COPING WITH PROBLEM BEHAVIORS

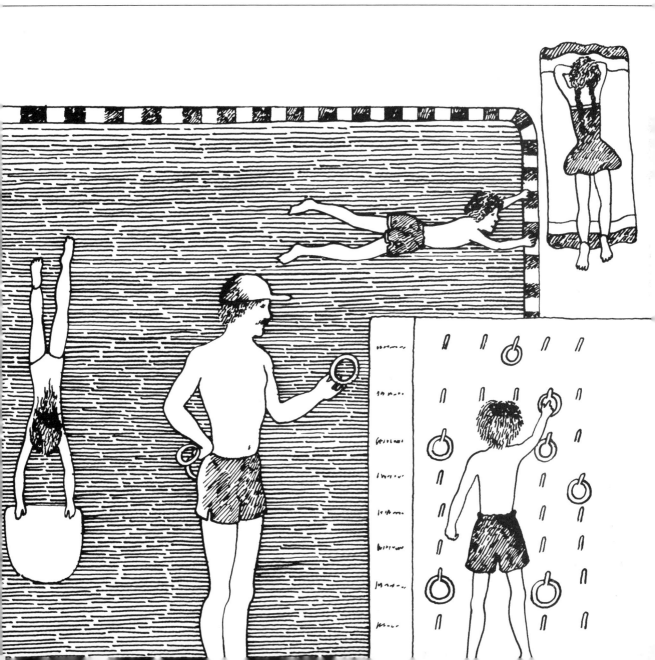

Objectives

Assuming you have mastered some source material on record keeping, principles of behavior (such as methods for providing students with feedback on their performance), and student motivation and management, on completing this activity you should be able to:

- Break your enabling objectives down into a series of recordable subtasks.

- Design a method for evaluating the accomplishment of these subtasks.

- Describe and illustrate record-keeping and feedback systems for your class, employing the principles described in the text.

- Select and describe appropriate procedures for

  reinforcing correct student responses
  avoiding problem behaviors
  coping with problem behaviors

- Begin thinking about an appropriate mode of instruction for the tasks you selected.

Record Keeping, Feedback, and Avoiding and Coping with Problem Behaviors

At this point you have mapped out the task analysis upon which an instructional sequence will eventually be built. You selected a challenging, interesting, and relevant educational goal and composed some instructional objectives to serve that goal. One of the objectives was broken down into its component enabling objectives and subtasks. The subtasks were analyzed to identify an appropriate starting place for instruction. Consideration was given to the entering behaviors and other prerequisite behaviors required for a student to accomplish the learning task successfully. You then looked more closely at your students so you could make an educated guess about the appropriateness of the task for them. You are prepared to make some adjustments in this structure, should this later become necessary.

Our attention now turns to the signposts of progress towards the instructional objective and the effect that the information these signposts convey may have upon students' performance. You will be asked to design a record-keeping system to provide feedback for both you and your students. The feedback system should serve several purposes—to provide information, to encourage sustained student effort, and to help avoid behavioral problems. To prepare you to cope with such problems should they occur, we'll ask you to have some procedures ready for dealing with such behaviors.

Monitoring student progress

It is essential that both the student and the instructor be constantly aware of the student's progress in relation to the objectives. For the instructor, this means assessing task difficulty and recording task completion. This is accomplished by keeping careful records. The feedback from such records enables the instructor to determine the effectiveness and efficiency of the instructional methods, and gives the student evidence of accomplishments. Here are some points to consider when planning your record-keeping and student-feedback systems.

Since very elaborate recording procedures may prove too time-consuming, teachers should *make the system as simple to use as possible*. Checklists, specific response categories, simple codes, and other shorthand methods can save a great deal of time and effort. Separate student and teacher records should be used only if absolutely necessary.

Many instructors who recognize the importance of record keeping are nevertheless tempted to wait until a phase of instruction is completed before assessing the students' progress. This can lead to problems, for when instructors have many students and several objectives to evaluate at one time, there is a strong tendency toward biased assessment. Greater emphasis may be placed on a student's recent behavior than on the pattern of performance as a whole; or only selected sequences of performance may be recalled, biasing the assessment of the student's actual progress. If you record the success or failure of each step as it occurs, you can spot problems as they arise. The accumulated records can be analyzed later for weakness and strength in the sequence. Therefore, it is important to *record in small steps and at regular intervals*.

If the student fails to progress, the burden of blame falls on the instruction—it's too difficult, too easy, or not interesting. Since regular evaluation highlights trouble spots, progress should be evaluated at every step and necessary procedural revisions in instruction made as required.

A feedback system provides the student with information about progress toward each instructional objective—how much has been done and how much is left to do. To know that half the tasks have been achieved can be an exciting experience, greatly encouraging a student whose energies are wearing thin. But to know what *is* half, the student must see what the whole entails. The complete set of requisite performances should be revealed to the student from the first. *Indicate from the beginning all the steps to be evaluated, thus providing the student with a complete description of the instructional objective.*

Seeing direct and immediate evidence of their accomplishments often reinforces students. When students participate in recording their achievements, such reinforcement is immediate. Therefore, *give the students access to progress records, and when possible involve them in the recording procedures.*

Students with histories of failure, shy students, and students who require extra practice become discouraged by competition. Rather than competitively pitting such students one against the other, give each student the opportunity to compare progress against earlier progress or against some objective criterion guideline. The guideline might indicate, for instance, the time-per-objective that the student should average to meet all the criteria of terminal performance by the final evaluation period. *The student's progress should be measured primarily against his or her own initial entering behaviors, or against some objective criterion.*

Your record-keeping system should be geared to the interests and developmental level of your students. Check over the class description to remind yourself of the characteristics of your particular class. Students (especially younger children) will be interested in unusual and innovative systems—and subsequently in their own achievements. *Try to make your system attractive and interesting.*

The following recording systems are designed to give you some ideas and to illustrate the points already described. Try to think of alternative media or more interesting formats as you examine each one.

Figure 3 *Bulletin-board system for recording completion of reading units. When a child can read a story aloud perfectly, the child tape-records it, has it approved, and records the progress by adding a petal to his or her flower. This system would require that the teacher date the petals when earned, or record the time of completion for each child on a separate checksheet.*

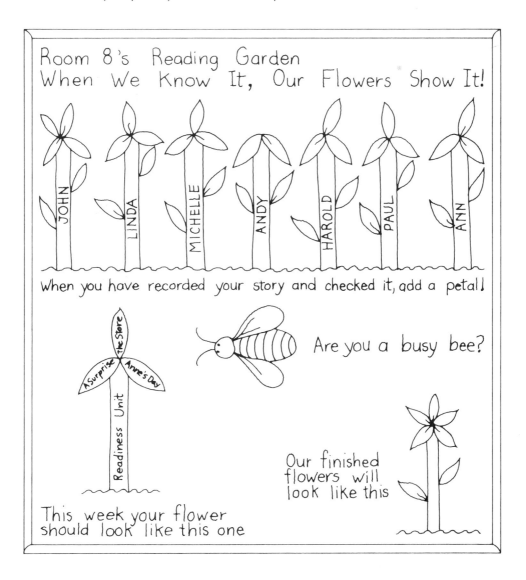

Figure 4 *A journal recording system. Below is a sample page from a science journal. The cover sheet for each experiment should include all pertinent information for grading. Collect books weekly for checks on progress and feedback, and for final assignment of grades at the end of the semester. If sheets are inserted for exam grades and comments, no separate records are necessary for these items.*

Biology Experiment 4

Date Begun:

Date Finished:

Summary:

Teacher's Comments:

Grade:

Figure 5 *A marker system. Team members move markers as appropriate. This system is a slightly more competitive system than the others. (Adapted from a study by McKenzie and Rushall, 1974.)*

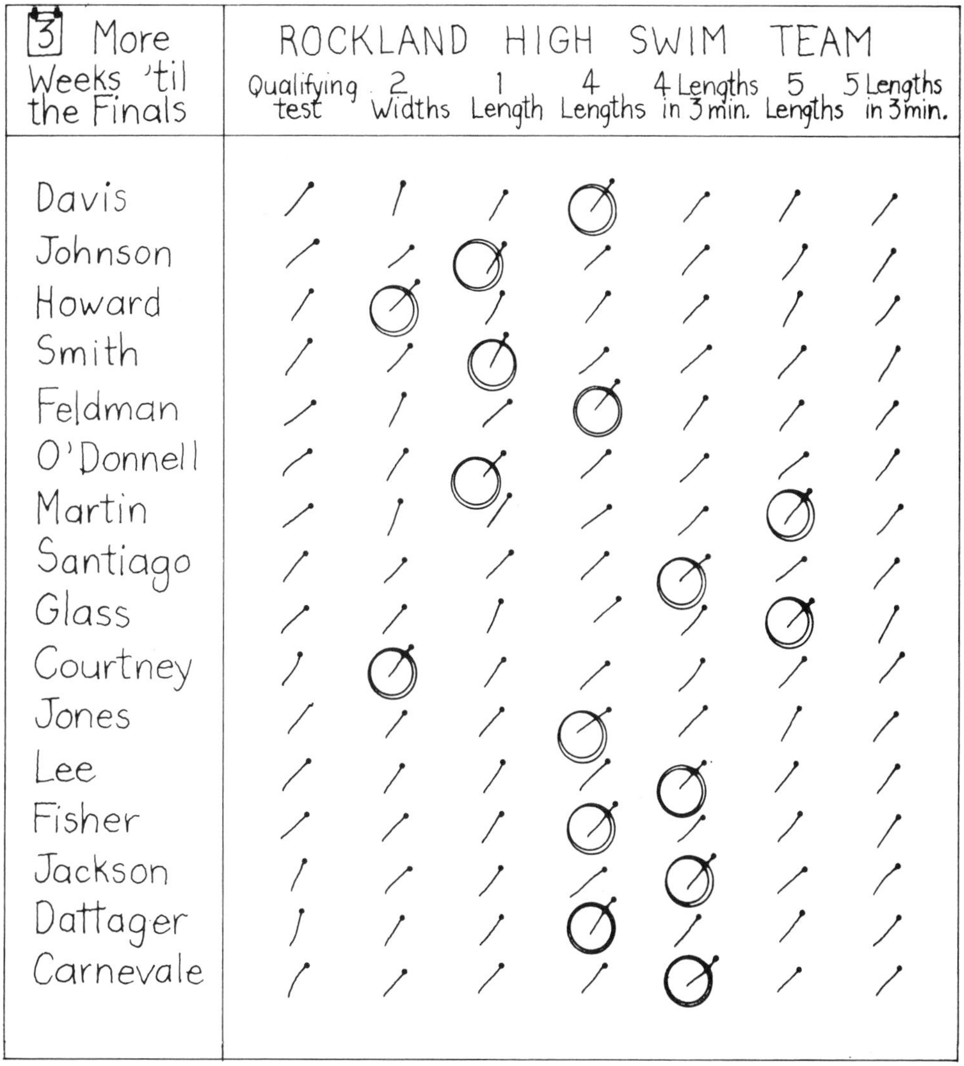

Figure 6 *Progress chart for a personalized system of instruction (PSI) course. The student marks the date each unit is completed.*

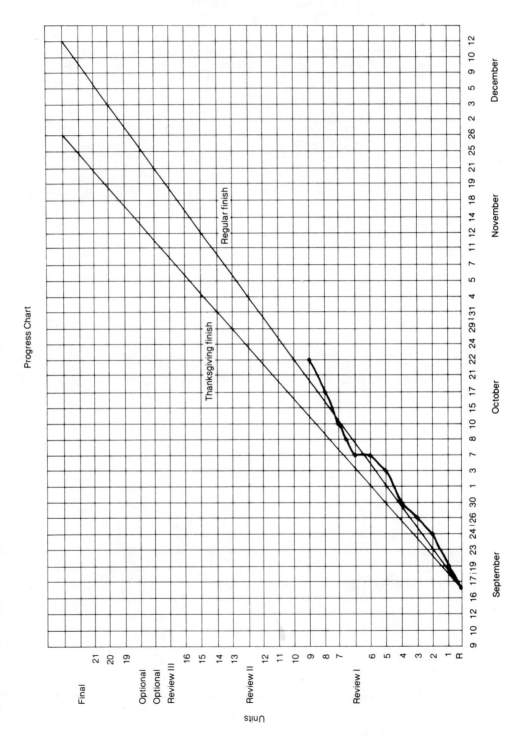

Progress Chart

4.1   Now it's your turn! List all the steps you will record as the student progresses through each subtask in your task analysis to the enabling objectives and finally to the instructional objective. Next to each step indicate how its accomplishment will be assessed. Try to use various forms of assessment, both formal and informal. Be innovative. Be certain the form you have chosen is appropriate in each case to the subtasks and enabling objectives you are evaluating.

Subtasks and Enabling Objectives	Assessment
_____	_____
_____	_____
_____	_____
_____	_____
_____	_____
_____	_____
_____	_____
_____	_____
_____	_____
_____	_____
_____	_____
_____	_____
_____	_____

4.2 Now design and illustrate, with a careful drawing, an original record-keeping and feedback system that will accurately indicate each student's progress through the steps you listed for Activity 4.1. (You will want to use a separate sheet or sheets of paper for this. If you prefer, you may actually construct the entire system—it might be more challenging!)

4.3 Describe the operation of your record-keeping system and relate it to the sequencing of your tasks. Explain where it will be located in the classroom (or other facility) and describe whether the students will participate in record keeping—and if so, how.

_____

_____

_____

_____

_____

_____

4.4 Put a check mark next to each quality if it is in your system.

a. Is your record-keeping system simple to use? _____

b. Are small steps recorded? _____

c. Does your system allow for frequent evaluation? _____

d. Does it provide a complete picture of all desired performances? _____

e. Is it readily accessible to students? _____

f. Do students actively participate in the system? _____

g. Does it provide an appropriate guideline against which students can measure progress? _____

h. Is it appropriate to the interests and developmental levels of your students? _____

Reinforcing correct responses

For many students, just the knowledge that they have responded correctly or acceptably is enough to keep them going. Effective teachers often say "right," or make some positive evaluative statement such as "That was an original, yet practical solution." Often a nod of agreement or a smile serves the same purpose. When students have a long history of failure in school or have developmental, social, or personal deficits or disabilities, being correct may not be a sufficiently strong reinforcer. In such cases, other stimuli should be delivered after each correct response, until the record of the student's performance indicates that being correct in itself encourages the responses. It is a good idea to proceed from such "natural" reinforcers as those already mentioned to some that are often practiced in schools—smiling faces, stars, access to special privileges—and ultimately, if none of the latter are effective, to such contrived reinforcers as food or prizes. It is important to pair the contrived reinforcers continually with praise and positive attention, so that once the appropriate response pattern is firmly established the instructor can *gradually* reduce and delay the delivery of "contrived" objects and events.

You should already have an idea whether or not simple natural reinforcers will provide adequate motivation for the students you described in Activity 3. (If you are not familiar with this aspect of your students' responding, visit a school and observe a similar population, or interview a teacher who has worked with a similar group.)

4.5 Now describe two ways you might reinforce correct student responses, being sure to describe how each will be administered.

a. _____

_____

b. _____

_____

Students may also be motivated to respond by participating in the selection of activities or interesting materials. Original response formats such as plays, puppet shows, debates, and games may help motivate them.

4.6   Describe in detail two or three other methods that might be appropriate to motivate your students.

a.   _____

_____

b.   _____

_____

c.   _____

_____

Avoiding problem behaviors

Students at any developmental level may show such problem behaviors as inattention, hostility, disruption, or destructiveness. Such behaviors often accompany one of several conditions that prevail in many schools.*

The instructional materials are not suited to the students. Material that is too difficult produces frustration and consequent emotional outbursts; material that is too easy produces boredom, encouraging the student to seek other forms of stimulation. Therefore, careful instructional planning, in addition to maximizing student learning, will also reduce problem behavior.

There are social conditions in the school that generate problem behavior. Some problems stem from peer behavior (such as teasing); others arise from the pupil-teacher relationship. Again, careful instructional planning tailored to the abilities and aspirations of individual students tends to minimize friction between students and teachers, since the student is accomplishing subtasks and the teacher is reinforcing the accomplishments. Peer conflicts will also be less frequent when each student is making effective progress and destructive competition is minimized.

*For an extensive treatment of this topic, see B. Sulzer and G. R. Mayer, *Behavior Modification Procedures for School Personnel* (Hinsdale, Ill.: The Dryden Press, 1972), and B. Sulzer-Azaroff and G. R. Mayer, *Applying Behavior Analysis Procedures with Children and Youth* (New York: Holt, Rinehart & Winston, 1977).

Students are seldom praised for good behavior. Working hard, cooperating with peers, interacting positively—these desirable school behaviors are, unfortunately, not likely to attract the instructor's attention as much as disturbing behaviors (not working, distracting others, dawdling, fighting). Yet teacher attention is a powerful reinforcer for most students. Teachers need to remind themselves of this fact. If you have a hard time remembering to notice good behavior, set yourself a goal—for example, "I'll be sure to catch at least five students (or groups) being good each hour"—and record each time you attain this goal. Outstanding teachers are constantly in motion, continually circulating about their classrooms to assist, encourage, and approve of their students; to catch them being good.

4.7   Refer to Activity 3.7, the student description. Guided by the students' characteristics, describe one procedure you plan to follow to avoid the development of problem behaviors.

a. The procedure _____

_____

b. The problem it should help you avoid _____

_____

_____

A student's behavior in school may be affected by all sorts of personal and social events buried in the past, inaccessible to current analysis. Persistent disruptive and destructive behaviors—in spite of careful design of instruction and appropriate reinforcement and delivery—call for some further planning. Here are some suggestions.

Analyze the undesirable behavior and identify, with the student's participation, some alternative constructive activities that are incompatible with the undesirable behavior. For example, working cooperatively with others on a biology experiment is not compatible with fighting. Then, finding (again with the student's cooperation) an appropriate reinforcer, deliver that reinforcer very frequently when the student is engaging in the desired behavior.

If possible, ignore minor disruptions—attention from teachers often serves as a reinforcer. Praise or nod approval to students who follow your lead in ignoring such minor disruptions. Pay lots of attention to the student working and behaving in a socially acceptable manner, and express approval to peers who show their approval of such a student.

Try a contracting system with the offending student. In private, work out a mutually agreeable system: for so many minutes of nondisruptive or on-task behavior, the student will receive in exchange so many privileges or rewards. (It is a good idea, if feasible, to involve parents, counselors, and supervisors in such planning.) If you are concerned that such a system may be considered unfair by the other students, consider these alternatives:

- Make reward delivery inconspicuous—after school or smoothly integrated into classroom routine.

- Use a daily report-card system, arranging for parents to deliver rewards or privileges as a consequence of a certain number of good behavior reports.

- Allow all the students to earn the more obvious rewards and privileges—each for some behavior she or he would like to increase.

- Occasionally give the rewards and privileges to the other students for free.

- Explain why you are doing what you are doing and solicit the other students' cooperation. (The offending student, after all, has been repeatedly rewarded with more than his or her share of attention.)

Try a group reward system. Allow the whole class or group to have access to some preferred activity for a given period of time as the reward for a selected accomplishment. Now you should make plans.

4.8 If you have problem behaviors (disruption, destructiveness) in your class, how do you plan to deal with them? Briefly describe two classroom behaviors that would interfere with learning and sketch a procedure you would use to eliminate each of them. (Try to select two different procedures.)

a. Behavior: _____

_____

Procedure: _____

_____

b. Behavior: _____

_____

Procedure: _____

_____

Since the next unit will ask you to organize your instructional sequence, this is a good time for you to begin to think about how you will proceed.

4.9　Choose an enabling objective, a subtask, or a short series of the sub-

tasks you listed in Activity 4.1. _____

_____

_____

Indicate how you might begin to teach the desired performances, using:

a. Programmed instruction (refer to Format 5.2) _____

_____

_____

b. Discussion (refer to Format 5.3) _____

_____

_____

c. Laboratory (refer to Format 5.4) _____

_____

_____

d. Demonstration (refer to Format 5.5) _____

_____

_____

e. Other format _____

_____

_____

You are ready at last for the biggest step—designing the instructional sequence itself. You have done most of the preliminary planning, as illustrated by your completion of the first four activities. Next you will design the lesson and later you will evaluate its effectiveness in your class or with a few sample students.

4.10 Write any comments or constructive suggestions you have about this activity.

_____

_____

_____

_____

SUPPLEMENTARY EXERCISES

1. Acquainting Yourself with Record-Keeping Systems

Purpose: To acquaint you with various record-keeping systems.

Below are listed several kinds of record-keeping systems. Select one or more to examine and evaluate.

1. *Records kept by teachers or students.* Interview a teacher and ask to see and discuss with that teacher: the methods used to record student progress in academic tasks and subtasks; legally required records such as attendance records; other records kept for the students' or for the teacher's own use; and student records. (Ask the instruc-

tor if the students in the class keep any records of their own progress. If so, describe them.)

2. *Record-keeping systems coordinated with textual material.* In the library you should be able to find some sets of teacher guides for instructional material. These guides frequently include descriptions of record-keeping systems. Find and describe a few of these.

3. *Counseling or advisement records.* Make an appointment with a pupil-service individual such as a guidance counselor, speech therapist, psychologist, or school social worker. Discuss with this person the aims or goals of the program and the record-keeping system used.

4. Comment on the records or the record-keeping systems that you have identified and make suggestions for improvement.

5. Include your own comments and suggestions.

2. Book or Chapter Report

Purpose: To add to your repertoire of information about classroom management or motivation.

Refer to the fourth supplementary exercise in Activity 3, "Planning for Students with Special Needs." Select a book or chapter on classroom management or motivation and complete the activities described in that exercise.

3. Literature Search for Motivation and Management Systems

Purpose: To familiarize you with current or recent journal articles in student motivation and management.

Go to the library and select a recently published journal that deals with education or applied behavioral psychology, such as the *Journal of Applied Behavior Analysis, Behavior Therapy,* the *Journal of Special Education,* the *Journal of Educational Psychology,* or *Exceptional Children.* Outline an article by completing a brief description of each of the following:

1. Introduction—what was the purpose of the study?

2. Why was this purpose designated? Upon what literature or previous findings was the study based?

3. Describe the methods used, the subjects who participated; the teachers, parents, or other personnel involved; the kind of data collected or measured and the procedure for its collection; other information about materials and environmental factors, such as a description of the physical setting; the method used to control extraneous factors that could affect the outcome; and the steps (in outline form) that were followed in the procedure.

4. Describe the *results* and how they were presented.

5. Summarize the discussion. Consider the outcome of the study and whether the purpose of the study was achieved.

6. Comment about how this study relates to your own experience, to materials you have been reading, and to other aspects of your career development.

4. Contingency Analysis

Purpose: To enable you to analyze, in a natura' setting, the antecedents and consequences that affect a behavior. (The technical term for such an analysis is *contingency analysis.*)

1. Visit a classroom or group instructional activity in a school, institution, or other facility for children or youths. Spend several hours watching for potential reinforcing activities and events. Try to list as many activities as you are able to observe

that appear to be reinforcing for some of the students—for example, special assignments, jobs, activities, and privileges.

2. Observe the students and determine if there are any other objects to which they might have access that would be reinforcing for them—such as school materials, books, games, or chalk.

3. List some of the social reinforcers that appear to be available in the situation, such as teacher or peer approval or attention.

4. Record some data about the interactions between students or clients and the teacher, instructor, trainer, or supervisor. Do this in the following way.

a. Take a sheet of paper and divide it into three columns—"Antecedents," "Behavior," and "Consequences."

b. Now select a student. List, about once a minute for about five minutes, each of the student behaviors that you observe.

c. Indicate in the "Antecedent" column what events occurred just before the behavior; in the "Behavior" column, the behavior itself; and in the "Consequences" column, the consequences delivered by the teacher, others, or the natural environment.

d. After five or so observations of this type, switch the order, so that now you are looking at the teacher (or other person interacting with the student). For the teacher's (or other's) behaviors, indicate the antecedent, those events that preceded the behavior, and the consequences—for example, the student response.

5. Discuss the relations among antecedents, behaviors, and consequences, in terms of increasing and maintaining constructive classroom activities.

6. Include your own comments and suggestions.

5. Observing Classroom Management and Motivation

Purpose: To provide you with the experience of measuring student-teacher interactions in an actual classroom to assess management and motivational variables.

1. Visit an instructional setting, as in the previous exercise, and spend about half an hour observing informally. After receiving your host's permission, identify the complete set of behaviors that constitute on-task and off-task behaviors. For example, on-task behaviors might include working with instructional material; writing assigned work; orienting towards the teacher; orienting towards a book; listening to a tape recorder; or viewing filmstrips. Off-task behaviors—behaviors that are incompatible with work—include walking around the room, staring out the window, or talking to other students about nontask activities.

2. Identify several students by name and list their names on a sheet of paper. Using a watch with a second hand, observe a student for ten seconds. If at any time during the ten-second interval the student is off-task, score the interval as a minus. If the student is on-task throughout the interval, score the interval as a plus. In the event that you're not sure whether the student is on- or off-task, score the interval as a question mark.

3. Within the five seconds following that interval, indicate what kinds of consequences are being delivered by the instructor. If the instructor is attending, put an *A* next to that interval.

4. Observe another student in the same manner, and continue recording for about ten minutes.

5. At the end of the recording session, count the number of on-task intervals recorded for each student in the class and the number of off-task and question intervals for each student. Also count the number of intervals during which the teacher gave attention. Specify the proportion of teacher attention given following on-task behavior and following off-task behavior.

6. Comment on the management procedure being used, based on the reading that you have done on classroom motivation and management.

6. Teacher Interview on Motivation and Management

Purpose: To enable you to share a teacher's perceptions of motivation and management problems.

Arrange with your instructor to interview a teacher; or, if you have a friend who is teaching or working in an instructional situation, arrange an interview at that person's convenience.

1. Discuss with that individual motivation and management problems and strengths in the group situation. Describe highly motivated students in the group. Describe motivational problems in the group. Describe situations in which students are unusually cooperative. Describe problems in group management.

2. Discuss with the teacher his or her methods for dealing with management and motivational problems, and for encouraging high rates of task completion and cooperative behaviors.

3. After the interview, consider some additional or alternative methods (based on your reading) that the teacher might use in increasing or enhancing high rates of productivity and cooperative behavior.

4. Include your own comments and suggestions.

7. Pupil Interview

Purpose: To enable you to share a student's perspectives on motivational and management issues.

1. Conduct an interview with a student at the secondary-school level or below.

2. Ask the student the questions given in the previous exercise.

3. Comment on the student's answers and suggest methods that the student and the teacher might use together to enhance productivity and cooperation in the learning situation.

4. Make your own comments and suggestions.

SUGGESTED READINGS AND REFERENCES

Anastasiow, N. *Educational Psychology: A Contemporary View.* Del Mar, Ca.: Communications Research Machines, 1973. Chapter 10, pp. 192–94 (token economy) and pp. 195–202 (handling problem behaviors).

Anderson, R. C., and Faust, G. W. *Educational Psychology: The Science of Instruction and Learning.* New York: Dodd, Mead & Co., 1973. Pp. 248–64 (social and tangible reinforcement, negative reinforcement and punishment, and extrinsic versus intrinsic reinforcement); pp. 270–95 (corrective feedback).

Becker, W. C.; Englemann, S.; and Thomas, D. R. *Teaching 1: Classroom Management.* Chicago: Science Research Associates, 1975. Units 5–10, pp. 94–202 (reinforcement); units 11–13, pp. 203–71 (token system, contract system, punishment); unit 16, pp. 301–11 (conduct problems).

Biehler, R. F. *Psychology Applied to Teaching.* Boston: Houghton Mifflin Co., 1971. Chapter 9, pp. 343–45 (merits of praise and blame).

Blair, G. M.; Jones, R. S.; and Simpson, R. H. *Educational Psychology.* New York: Macmillan Co., 1975. Chapter 7, pp. 182–91 (providing the student with feedback), 174–77 (reinforcement), and 195–98 (applying reinforcement strategically); chapter 19, pp. 510–34 (advantages and disadvantages of pupil placement).

Bushell, D., Jr. *Classroom Behavior.* Englewood Cliffs, N.J.: Prentice-Hall, 1973. Chapter 3, pp. 35–47 (record keeping of progress and achievement); chapter 5, pp. 71–79 (eliminating problem behavior); chapter 6, pp. 83–99 (reinforcement and the token system).

DeCecco, J. P., and Crawford, W. E. *The Psychology of Learning and Instruction.* Englewood Cliffs, N.J.: Prentice-Hall, 1974. Chapter 7, pp. 187–88 (reinforcement as feedback); chapter 9, pp. 259–64 (feedback).

Gage, N. L., and Berliner, D. C. *Educational Psychology.* Chicago: Rand McNally College Publishing Co., 1975. Unit 17, pp. 335–39 (feedback such as verbal praise and social rewards).

Givner, A., and Graubard, P. S. *A Handbook of Behavior Modification For The Classroom.* New York: Holt, Rinehart & Winston, 1974. Chapter 1, pp. 1–22 (eight guidelines on developing reinforcement systems for effective instruction); chapter 2, pp. 25–54 (the token economy); chapter 3, pp. 59–82 (alternatives to the token economy).

Hamachek, D. E. *Behavior Dynamics in Teaching, Learning, and Growth.* Boston: Allyn & Bacon, 1975. Chapter 10, pp. 450–56 (reinforcement and punishment); chapter 11, pp. 497–99 (praise and criticism).

Klausmeier, H. J., and Goodwin, W. *Learning and Human Abilities: Educational Psychology.* 4th ed. New York: Harper & Row, Publishers, 1966. Chapter 15, pp. 402–46 (behavior problems and how to handle them).

Lefrancois, G. R. *Psychology for Teaching.* Belmont, Ca.: Wadsworth Publishing Co., 1975. Chapter 3, pp. 51–54 (reinforcement and punishment and their effects).

McKenzie, T. L., and Rushall, B. R. "Effects of Self-Recording on Attendance and Performance in a Competitive Swimming Training Environment." *Journal of Applied Behavior Analysis* 7 (1974): 199–206.

Meacham, M. L., and Wiesen, A. E. *Changing Classroom Behavior.* 2nd ed. New York: Intext Educational Publishers, 1974. Part 1, pp. 25–56 (strengthening desirable behaviors) and pp. 63–78 (eliminating undesirable behaviors); part 2, pp. 131–75 (application in the normal classroom).

Smith, M. D. *Educational Psychology and Its Classroom Applications.* Boston: Allyn & Bacon, 1975. Chapter 10, pp. 289–90 (feedback).

Sulzer, B., and Mayer, G. R. *Behavior Modification Procedures for School Personnel.* Hinsdale, Ill.: The Dryden Press, 1972, Part 1, pp. 21–61 (increasing the occurrence of existing behaviors); part 4, pp. 135–216 (reducing or eliminating the occurrence of undesirable behaviors).

Sulzer-Azaroff, B., and Mayer, G. R. *Applying Behavior Analysis Procedures with Children and Youth.* New York: Holt, Rinehart & Winston, 1977.

Taber, J. I.; Glaser, R.; and Schaefer, H. H. *Learning and Programmed Instruction.* Reading, Mass.: Addison-Wesley Publishing Co., 1965. Chapter 2, pp. 22–28 (reinforcement); chapter 8, pp. 169–70 (reinforcement).

5
DESIGNING AN INSTRUCTIONAL SEQUENCE

Objectives

Assuming that you have read and mastered information on teaching models and on designing instructional materials, on completing this activity you should be able to:

- Choose a specific set of materials and instructional procedures to use in teaching the tasks you have chosen.

- Describe two alternatives to your chosen teaching style, and reasons why you have chosen the method you are using in preference to others.

- Design an instructional sequence to teach a specific enabling objective or specific subtasks, incorporating the properties of:
  logical sequencing
  relevance and effectiveness of instructional stimuli to the
      students' interests and aspirations
  active student involvement
  appropriate feedback
  reinforced progress

Designing an Instructional Sequence

This is the activity you've been waiting for! Now you will select your actual teaching materials and design a set of specific instructional procedures. A particularly effective approach is to apply rules based on the empirical discoveries or "principles" of learning and instruction. Such an approach can be used for almost any classroom topic or format. Do not feel limited to standard or "normal" classroom procedures; the range of possibilities is as broad as your imagination.

There are certain criteria you should consider when planning for *any* lesson. They are as essential to the educational success of a field trip as they are to a lecture or questioning sequence.

- *The instruction should be logically sequenced so that each activity or subtask leads to the next.* Organization—rather than a random sequence of activities—is the key. The component parts of the sequence should form a cohesive whole. Carefully organized instruction does not, however, imply inflexibility. Rather, it provides a framework upon which varied experiences may rest. Let us use as an example the impact of industrialization on other social structures. Suppose a sequence of subtasks were selected that involved students' doing library research, reading textbooks, and writing about the impact of industrialization on such institutions as the schools, the courts, and the family. One student has recently returned from living abroad in a country undergoing industrialization and in the midst of her class work realizes that her experiences and observations are quite relevant. She would like to do a slide presentation for the class. Another student has been following a series of news articles on the role of the family in nations at various levels of industrialization. He would like to follow up that interest by preparing an annotated scrapbook to place in the class library. Each of these activities is not only appropriate, but highly desirable; because a sequential structure of instruction has been designed, they are relevant and can easily be integrated into the concepts the students are learning.

• *Your instructional stimuli should be designed for maximum effectiveness and appropriateness.* Instructional stimuli are those objects or events designed to cue particular student responses. Books, lab manuals, workbooks, verbal presentations, and discussion outlines provide appropriate situations for such student responses as answering questions, writing reports, and doing projects. Other material—such as lab specimens, checklists, films, slides, tapes, charts, displays, sets of objects in or outside the classroom, and rearrangements of the physical environment—allow for more varied forms of response.

Several qualities should enhance the effectiveness of the instructional stimuli. First, they should be *related to the instructional objective.* Tangential material should be kept to a minimum. Second, instructional stimuli should be *clear and precise.* The type of response desired from the students should be apparent to them; they should not have to guess. A workbook question, for example, should be specific. You wouldn't ask a student to write "five hundred words on what you know about biology" when what you really want to know is whether the student can list the phyla or describe the life cycle of a fern. *Instructional stimuli should maximize the likelihood of correct responding*—if necessary through the use of artificial cues or *prompts,* though such prompts gradually should be removed. Kinds of prompts you can use are: *hints* ("It's a country in South America"); *rhymes* ("If *sip* becomes *sipped,* then *trip* becomes _____"); or *pictures* illustrating the desired response. (See the format on programmed instruction for other types of prompts.)

Instructional stimuli should be selected to *generate responses appropriate to the student's behavioral repertoire.* You'd only ask a student to draw a picture of the slide under a microscope if that student could operate a microscope and draw reasonable facsimiles. Moreover, appropriate instructional stimuli are related to the students' interests or are inherently interesting. For instance, if your students come from Latino backgrounds, examples can be drawn from that culture. As you attempt to use stimuli that are related to your students' interests, it is a good idea to communicate to the individuals in your class the relevance to them of the topic you have chosen. When you capitalize on the students' present interests and future aspirations, they are more attentive and involved. Emphasize their special talents. If you want them to write poetry, let musically inclined students write lyrics to rock or folk songs. If they like to sing, let them sing their poetry recitations. Individually contracting with students about their mode of participation is a highly appropriate strategy.

• *The students should be actively involved in the instruction!* This involvement can serve many purposes. First, it enables the learner to acquire complex material more effectively. Second, it commands and holds the attention of the learners. Third, active responding can be used to direct students' attention to a certain type of content. If you frequently ask for quotations of names and dates, students will selectively attend to such material in their reading. If you want them to be able to summarize a paragraph, having them list the basic points of a paragraph will direct their attention to the essential material.

Active participation in the instruction also enables students to practice and to be reinforced for the appropriate response until it is well established. Give students some practice in making responses similar to those for which they will be evaluated. The response may be made in a different mode—perhaps orally rather than in writing—but it should require the same level of complexity or sequences of subskills desired in the terminal behavior. For example, if you are teaching students to communicate in idiomatic French, you would have them speak idiomatic French, listen to and translate it, or draw and label cartoons using it, rather than having them research the origins of the idioms or write an idiom fifty times.

The active involvement of the students also provides information about the adequacy of the instruction. For example, inappropriate student responses may indicate that a particular concept has not been clearly formulated. If some aspect of the performance is deficient, more instructional time and relevant practice can be allotted to the necessary subtasks. Instructional sequences can be revised to incorporate additional material or to eliminate redundant instruction.

• *The sequence (as discussed in Activity 4) should provide informative feedback so students can evaluate the adequacy of their responses.* Sometimes referred to as "knowledge of results," this information about the adequacy of performance should be provided as quickly as possible. Evidence suggests that feedback that is seriously delayed loses its effectiveness for the learner. A simple, effective method is to supply the appropriate feedback immediately following the student response.

Success is immediately reinforcing; failure can result in discouragement and subsequent loss of interest. In order to generate and maintain high levels of performance and to maximize success and minimize failure, *progress toward the instructional objective should be reinforced along the way.* The technique of "shaping" is a good example of the application of this principle. In shaping, each performance that more closely resembles the terminal behavior is reinforced, beginning with the entering behavior and progressing through a graduated series of behavioral steps to the goal behavior. Proper sequencing of instruction from the simple to the complex provides the essential basis for such techniques. However, try to make the material challenging enough so students are encouraged to progress.

A number of instructional formats are included in this activity. Each illustrates how you can incorporate the preceding suggestions into several types of instructional sequence. The formats range from a general, flexible format to programmed instruction (a formal structuring of instruction that incorporates principles of behavior), and include such other exciting possibilities as student-designed formats, plays, experiments, and trips. Each is designed to assist you in planning an instructional sequence that is not only interesting but also effective in guiding your students as they progress toward the instructional objective. You will be asked to select one format or to design one of your own, and to describe the specific instructional activities in which students will engage. The next activity will give you the chance to carry out, evaluate, and revise the sequence you have designed.

You will probably be working on many instructional objectives during the course of a lesson or school day. Psychomotor, affective, and cognitive behaviors occur concurrently in a student's daily activities; each of these activities will thus help in achieving several objectives. While the students are working in groups on a science project, for instance, they may also be developing a preference for sharing ideas with one another rather than working alone.

Since this may be your first attempt at selecting and organizing instructional materials, you should try to accomplish only one or a few of the subtasks from your enabling objectives. When you actually use this plan professionally, it probably will be only one of a group of instructional activities organized around a more complete set of objectives. At that time, you will probably plan to achieve several instructional objectives in many of your lessons. The procedures will be analogous, with each objective considered carefully at the appropriate time in a manner similar to the one you will use now.

All students should complete Activities 5.1–5.5 plus *one* format. Students may choose *any one* of the six formats presented here or may arrange with their instructor to use a format of their choice.

5.1 a. As a reminder to be realistic in your planning, briefly describe your students' ages and development, backgrounds, strengths, weaknesses, interests, and likely duration of sustained effort. Plan instruction for *less* time than the maximal amount of time for which your students can sustain their efforts.

_____

_____

_____

b. The approximate duration of this instruction will be _____ minutes.

5.2 Write the goal for this particular instructional sequence. (This may include one or several subtasks.)

a. The verb phrase that describes what the student(s) will be doing (observable, measurable response) upon completion of the sequence: _____

_____

b. Under what conditions?

1. Describe setting, room, or facilities. _____

_____

2. With what tools and materials? _____

_____

3. With what instructions? _____

_____

4. With whose assistance? _____

_____

5. Restrictions: without what materials, instructions, or assistance?

_____

6. Other conditions or restrictions? _____

_____

c. To what level of proficiency? _____

_____

5.3 a. How will you communicate the *goals* of the instructional sequence to your students? Explain how your students will know what is expected of them. Check the appropriate items.

Demonstration of the terminal behavior _____

Sample test questions _____

Written copy of the course objectives _____

Oral description and explanation _____

Other (describe briefly) _____

_____

b. Write the steps you will follow to accomplish 5.3a. (Attach sample items, a copy of your written description, or a script, if appropriate.) _____

_____

_____

_____

5.4 a. How will you communicate to the students the *relevance* of the enabling objective or subtask(s) to the instructional objective? How will you relate the goals to their own interests and aspirations?

Explanation by instructor _____

"Drawing out" inferences from the students themselves _____

Demonstration, field trip _____

Other (describe briefly) _____

_____

_____

b. Write down your explanation, inference, or demonstration, including questions. (You may attach additional sheets of paper.)

_____

_____

_____

_____

Skim through the suggested formats and decide which is most appropriate to use in teaching your particular enabling objective or subtask(s). Then you have two options. The first option is to complete one of the formats provided. You may wish to try several and then choose the approach that suits you best. This is particularly advisable if you are unfamiliar with some of the types of suggested sequences. Although we have provided specific topical formats to aid you in designing a range of instructional sequences using various techniques, you have a second option—to employ a different style. A list of suggested alternatives is included with the formats. The general considerations are common to all, so *feel free to develop your own format*. Should you do so, review the four basic points discussed under "Designing an Instructional Sequence" plus all relevant items included in the general format, and offer a rationale for choosing an alternative format.

5.5 a. List *three* formats you feel might be appropriate to your goal, and explain why you think each would be appropriate.

1. _____

_____

2. _____

_____

3. _____

_____

b. Place an asterisk next to the format you have selected and explain its advantage over the other two.

_____

_____

5.6 What types of stimuli will you use for presentation of the instructional material? (If possible, bring these materials to show your instructor.)

a. Films _____
Reading text _____
Lecture _____
Plays _____
Experiment _____
Games _____
Discussion outline _____
Personalized system of instruction (PSI) _____
Discovery learning method _____
Teacher- or student-prepared materials (describe) _____

_____

Other alternatives _____

b. Give titles of any films, records, or texts you will use. For demonstrations, identify the demonstrator and how you will locate him or her. Be specific about all the resource and instructional materials you will need. (Remember that these must usually be arranged for in advance of the actual lesson.)

_____

_____

_____

_____

c. Here is an opportunity to use your originality and creativity to conceptualize and carry out the preparation of some instructional materials. If you're considering a game format, you might design a game board or cards; for a trip, maps, trip diaries, or study guides; for a discussion, pictures, slides, or audio tapes to stimulate the discussion. While you should not have to spend an inordinate amount of time on the preparation of materials, those of you who are inclined to do so will find this an enjoyable and instructive activity. (Bring these materials along to show your instructor, if possible.)

d. Write down any examples or illustrations that you will use.

_____

_____

_____

e. List any instructions the students will need before you can begin

instruction. _____

_____

_____

_____

Possible formats for your instructional sequence include the following:

Formats for which specific forms have been included:

5.1   General format
5.2   Programmed instruction
5.3   Discussion group
5.4   Laboratory: experiments and other problem-solving activities
5.5   On-site: games, field trips, simulations, role playing
5.6   Student-designed format

Formats that you might like to design yourself:

Interviews
Guest lectures (this should be highly structured)
Contracts for specific activities
Individual presentations or seminars
Scripts for a videotape lesson
Panel discussions
Debates
Puppet shows
Songs
Art projects
Dances
Contests
Journals
Book reviews
Field experiences
Independent study
Individualized instruction

Now go ahead and complete your selected format.

FORMAT 5.1

GENERAL FORMAT FOR DEVELOPING AN INSTRUCTIONAL SEQUENCE

5.1.1　How will you provide for active and relevant student responses?

    a. What forms of response are most appropriate as practice for the desired terminal behavior (answering questions, skill performance, individual presentations)? Write specific examples below.

_____

_____

_____

_____

_____

_____

_____

_____

    b. List approximately five appropriate cues to signal these responses (questions, instructions, gestures—be specific).

1. _____

2. _____

3. _____

4. _____

5. _____

c. If students are unable to make the responses, list three ways you will prompt them; include a sample of each.

1. _____

_____

2. _____

_____

3. _____

_____

_____

5.1.2 How will students receive and use informative feedback?

a. List three forms of feedback you will employ during the instruction and illustrate each in terms of your lesson. (Answers from the teacher, exchange of papers for immediate grading, students' checking their answers against text, or posting test results are some possibilities.) Indicate when the feedback will occur relative to the responses.

1. _____

_____

2. _____

_____

3. _____

_____

_____

b. Suggest how the results of feedback will be used by the student. (Will the student redesign the experiments, take a second mastery quiz, explain the idea more fully to classmates?)

_____

_____

_____

_____

_____

5.1.3 Organize all the procedures you have described into an orderly sequence. List this sequence of procedures in outline form. Indicate _when_ the students will be doing what; _where_ response and feedback sequences will occur; _what_ the teacher will be doing; _when_ each presentation question or explanation will be given; and approximately how much time is planned for each activity. Here is a brief example:

Instructional objective: Given a series of assigned readings, discussions, and field trips, the student should be able to offer an explanation of at least three of the major sources of ecological imbalance produced by man.

Enabling objective: Given discussions and a series of experiments, students can provide a detailed description of the threats to waterfowl presented by oil spillage.

I. Introduction _(ten minutes)_
   A. Ask questions about pollution and ecology, exploring the students' general familiarity with the subject (informal preassessment).
   B. Encourage comments on the relevance of ecology (help students perceive the purpose of instruction).
      1. Reinforce with smiles and positive comments when a student explains a tie between pollution and personal experience.
      2. Offer some examples of the importance of sound ecological practices.

C. Pass out a list of topics (subtasks) for next week's study. Have the students check off the enabling objective they will concentrate on today (for example, to be able to describe the effects of oil slicks on waterfowl).
   1. Give a demonstration, incorporating examples of the performance of the enabling objective you are teaching today, and explaining its relevance to the instructional objective (for example, show a short film clip on the experiences of waterfowl with oil slicks).
   2. Have one or two students summarize the film clip. Praise when appropriate.

II. Have students conduct an experiment *(twenty minutes)* involving the flotation of various objects in clear and then in oily water.
   A. Give complete instructions and designate groups.
   B. Allow time for a practice performance by students.
      1. Circulate among the students, reinforcing them for intergroup discussions and analysis of performances.
      2. Provide additional instruction or clarification for slower groups; provide suggestions or information if needed.

III. Large group interaction *(fifteen minutes)*
   A. Have groups describe or demonstrate the results of their experiment.
      1. Encourage classmate responses; reinforce heavily for positive comments and constructive criticism.
      2. Comment and give alternative positive suggestions following negative criticism by classmates of a student's description.

IV. Individual responses *(fifteen minutes)*
   A. Have each student write a short report on the experiment.
   B. Have students exchange papers and assess one another's work; return the papers to the writers and have them record the assessments in their journals.

V. Summary *(five minutes)*
   A. Group reassembles; you refer to today's enabling objective.
   B. Ask students to volunteer a summary of what was accomplished to illustrate the enabling objective.
   C. Write key phrases on the board.
   D. Compliment the class on what it has accomplished.

Now write your instructional sequence on this page. (Please print or type. Feel free to add extra pages.)

5.1.4 Show your questions, the appropriate responses, and (if possible) your instructional materials to your instructor. These materials should be properly organized and labeled so you are ready to conduct the instruction for the next activity.

5.1.5 Check the materials and outline you have against the following criteria. Add any comments you feel are relevant.

a. Is the instruction *sequenced logically?* _____

b. Are your *instructional stimuli* likely to be effective and appropriate? _____ Do they occasion responses appropriate to the students' behavioral repertoires? _____

c. Have you specified the *materials* you will use? _____

d. Is instruction keyed to the *interests and aspirations* of your students? _____

e. Have you provided for *active* response by the students? _____

f. Will you employ several forms of *informational feedback* (at least two)? _____

g. Is the feedback provided

frequently? _____
with minimal delay? _____
consistently? _____
often as an appropriate response following the student response? _____

h. Is progress toward the objective *reinforced* along the way?
_____

5.1.6 Write any comments or suggestions you have about Activity 5 and Format 5.1.

_____

_____

FORMAT 5.2

PROGRAMMED-INSTRUCTION FORMAT

Objectives

Assuming that you have read material (preferably a text) on programmed instruction and have looked at a few sample instructional programs, on completing this format you should be able to:

- List and illustrate six essential attributes of programmed instruction.

- Select several student responses relevant to the acquisition of a given instructional objective.

- Prepare informational and motivational feedback appropriate to a given student population and instructional objective.

- Divide the material designed to teach an instructional objective into a logical series of small units.

- Conceptualize and apply several prompting strategies.

- Reduce prompts gradually in such a way that by the end of the program the student relies totally on the instructional material and not on prompts at all.

- Assemble an instructional program containing approximately twenty-five frames.

Designing programmed instruction is a highly sophisticated skill. This format will familiarize you with the general methods involved, but you should realize that you are not likely to perform a professional job as an instructional programmer as a result of completing this format. For reading material on programmed instruction, see the Suggested Readings for Format 5.2 at the end of Activity 5.

Programmed Instruction

Programmed instruction is based on principles of behavior, particularly those principles that relate to the acquisition of new behavior. This system was originated by B. F. Skinner, who has written extensively on the topic. The basic philosophy of teaching behind the programmed-instruction format is trial and success; in other words, students' errors are minimized. This is accomplished by including the following steps in instruction.

Provision is made for frequent active student participation, often through written response, but occasionally through motor, oral, or other response. Here is an example:

> Programmed instruction provides for _____ _____ _____. (Fill in the blanks. Turn to page __ for the correct answers.)

Feedback as to the correctness of the response is provided immediately. This is done by presenting the correct answer on a different page or by providing some other form of guidance or criterion by which the correctness or appropriateness of the response can be assessed by the student. The answer to the example above, *"active student responding,"* might be placed on the following page or elsewhere in the text where it is accessible to the student. This time let's illustrate with a noncognitive instructional objective—forming clay into an object by rolling, cutting, and draping it over a form.

Instructions:

> Take a ball of clay and roll it out into a circle with a 7-inch diameter. The rolled clay should be of uniform thickness, approximately ¼ inch.

Feedback:

> Take a pin and stick it into the clay. Note the depth that the pin penetrates. Now repeat this at other spots on the circle, measuring the uniformity of thickness over the entire surface. If the pin penetrates to the same depth at each probe, you have rolled out a uniform slab.

Instructional material is presented in small steps or units. Instead of presenting a series of concepts (as in a textbook) or a page or two of information (as in a laboratory manual), information is usually limited to either a single, or at most a few points. The *frame,* or bit of instruction, is illustrated in the preceding examples by the material enclosed in boxes. An alternative would be to present a full paragraph or two containing a general point plus one or more illustrations. In either case, some active student response is required. In the latter instance, a multiple-choice question is often the preferred format. Here is an example:

Select the correct response.
  Programmed instruction:
    1. presents instructional information in small amounts. (page 33)
    2. always uses small frames. (page 26)
    3. can only be used to teach cognitive objectives. (page 29)

The student selects an answer and turns to the page indicated. Were the student to turn to page thirty-three, he or she might find the following written there: "Good for you. You did understand that one of the essential aspects of programmed instruction is that it presents its material in small units. It is this aspect of programmed instruction that enhances the likelihood that the student will learn successfully, while making progress towards the ultimate instructional objective."

If, on the other hand, the student had selected the third answer and turned to page twenty-nine, he or she might read something like this: "You selected an answer that indicates that programmed instruction can only be used to teach cognitive objectives. But do you remember that when the component *active student responding* was discussed, a motor response—rolling clay—was used as an illustration? Other motor responses, such as woodwork, laboratory experiments, setting up circuitry boards, or even penmanship, can be taught through programmed instruction."

Programmed instruction is prepared so that errors are minimized and correct responses are maximized. We have already seen one way in which this is accomplished: the use of small steps. A second method is the use of prompts or hints. Prompts are used in the early stages in the instructional sequence and are gradually removed until by the end of the sequence none are left. There are many types of prompts, some artificial, others natural. A good guideline is to use whatever prompts guarantee correct responding in the beginning, while trying as early as possible to use natural prompts. Here is another instance in which the student's behavioral repertoire plays a major role. If the student is ready for natural prompts (such as those related to the material itself), that is where instruction should begin. If not, one needs to devise some artificial prompts—even if they appear gimmicky—to guarantee initial success. The following section describes and illustrates various techniques.

Headings:

> Heading
> The first prompt described here draws the reader's attention to a key word. This is done by providing a _____.

Fill in the Blank:

> This is a ___ __ __ ____ prompt. The important factor with this kind of prompt is that the length of the lines hints at the number and length of the words.

Missing Letters:

> Even more guidance is given when the specific number of missing __ __ __ __ __ __ __ is provided. To practically guarantee correctness, one can start at an earlier approximation and even provide some of the key l__ __ __ t __ __ __.

Repetitions:

> Another sure-fire method to enhance correctness is to provide the correct response in the early part of a frame and ask the student to _repeat_ the response in a subsequent part. To be extra sure, in this example we have underlined the word we want the student to
>
> _____.

Building on General Information:

> One technique that is frequently used in programmed instruction is to request a response that is fairly certain to be answered correctly by anyone responding. For example, a frame might contain the following: "When an actor forgets his lines, he is assisted by a _____er. In programmed instruction *prompts* are also used to evoke the correct response."

Pictures:

 are used from time to time to prompt correct responses. Here a _____ prompt is illustrated.

Rhymes:

> If you want right answers most of the time, one way to get them is with a _____.

Synonyms:

> To provide conditions for trial and success, prompting helps the student to give the right or c_____ answer.

Antonyms:

> The old way of teaching was through trial and error, but programming teaches through trial and _____.

Questions:

This section discusses ways to use prompts in programmed instruction. Why is it frequently useful to provide such prompts?

Multiple Choice:

Prompts are:
a. used in equal amounts in all frames in a sequence.
b. used only towards the end of an instructional sequence.
c. are used heavily in early parts of a sequence, are gradually changed from artificial to natural, and are finally faded completely by the end of the sequence.

Context Setting:

Context setting also tends to make use of general knowledge. For instance, if the materials mentioned include cake, candles, and presents, it is fairly apparent that a _____ party is being discussed. When the discussion relates to methods of applying principles of the acquisition of behaviors to assist students to achieve a specific instructional objective, it is fairly obvious that i_____ is being discussed.

These are but a few of the prompting methods that have been used by instructional programmers. Anyone who makes the serious professional decision to program instruction must read source material on the topic and apply the methods for testing its effectiveness. You'll notice that some of the preceding prompts are arranged to make the commission of errors almost impossible.

5.2.1   Select two prompting methods and explain why they would tend to guarantee success. _____

_____

_____

_____

5.2.2   There are other prompting techniques that provide far less support. Give an example from the list above, and explain why you have selected it.

_____

_____

_____

_____

Provision is made for periodic review. Include frames later in the program that review earlier bits of information, but with fewer prompts.

Just as prompts are an integral part of programmed instruction, so is the requirement that those prompts eventually be faded until they are eliminated entirely. Usually the last frame of the sequence asks for a demonstration that the instructional objective has been achieved by the student—without offering any prompts or hints. Here is an example:

List and illustrate five characteristics of programmed instruction.

Programmed instruction is empirically based. This means that the final product has been field tested with a large sample of the population for which it was designed. Usually instructional programs go through a series of revisions as error patterns are analyzed and frames added, changed, and deleted or as sequences of frames are changed around. In addition to sequential analysis, attainment of the instructional objective is usually measured by a posttest.

A fully tested instructional program demonstrates its ability to teach a given population a set of specific instructional objectives more efficiently and more thoroughly than alternative methods. (Since this format is intended as an exercise only, a full empirical demonstration will not be required. You will, however, be asked to present and evaluate an instructional sequence in Activity 6.)

Now it is your turn to proceed through the steps of preparing a programmed instructional sequence. (Reread the preceding section on programmed instruction before you begin.)

5.2.3   Write the enabling objective or subtask towards which the program is directed. You may use the same enabling objective or subtask(s) you used earlier, or choose another one from your task analysis.

_____

_____

5.2.4   Compose the last frame in the sequence that will demonstrate that the student has attained the enabling objective or subtask(s). This frame should have no prompts.

_____

_____

_____

5.2.5   Write the correct answer to 5.2.4. _____

_____

5.2.6   Briefly describe the population of students for whom this program is designed (no need to give an elaborate description, since that was done earlier).

_____

_____

5.2.7 Compose an initial frame that essentially guarantees success for the group you have selected to teach. Under the frame, supply the correct answer.

a. Frame: _____

_____

_____

b. Feedback: _____

_____

5.2.8 On separate sheets of paper or on a set of index cards, prepare a sequence of programmed-instruction frames, starting with the frame you just composed and moving forward *in a logical sequence*. Provide many prompts at first and gradually diminish the prompts until the final frame is reached. Number each frame. Try to make your material interesting. (To get some ideas for your frames, take a look at some programmed-instruction materials at the library curriculum materials center, or ask your instructor to help you locate such materials.) Be creative! Since this assignment may appear deceptively simple, it is a good idea to include no more than twenty-five frames. Use this checklist to assess the adequacy of your initial writing. (Later you should try out the program with one student, note errors, revise the program, and re-present it to a second student, and so on with a number of students.)

5.2.9 Does each frame or bit of instruction involve the student actively?

a. Yes _____ No _____

b. How? _____

_____

_____

5.2.10 Are answers and other feedback provided?

    a. Yes _____ No _____

    b. Where are correct answers located? _____

    _____

    _____

5.2.11 Is information presented logically in small steps?

    a. Yes _____ No _____

    b. Describe the guidelines you used for designing each frame.

    _____

    _____

    _____

5.2.12 Did you use a variety of prompts?

    a. Yes _____ No _____

    b. List the types of prompts you used and identify the frame number
    for each type of prompt.

Prompt	Frame Number
_____	_____
_____	_____
_____	_____
_____	_____

5.2.13 Did you provide for periodic review? Yes _____ No _____

5.2.14 Did you gradually fade the prompts? Yes _____ No _____

5.2.15 Which frames are most heavily prompted?

_____

5.2.16 Which make use of artificial or contrived prompts?

_____

5.2.17 Which use natural prompts? _____

_____

5.2.18 Which use almost no prompts? _____

_____

You have now reached the most exciting part of this format: trying, evaluating, and revising your instructional program. You should feel proud!

5.2.19 Write any suggestions or constructive comments you have about Activity 5 and Format 5.2.

_____

_____

_____

_____

_____

_____

_____

FORMAT 5.3 _____

DISCUSSION FORMAT

5.3.1   Choose an enabling objective, subtask, or series of subtasks with which you feel thoroughly familiar. Write it down in final form.

_____

_____

_____

5.3.2   Support your selection of a *discussion* as an appropriate format to achieve this enabling objective or subtask.

_____

_____

_____

5.3.3   Refer to 5.3.1 and identify three to eight subordinate goals for the discussion.

a. _____

b. _____

c. _____

d. _____

e. _____

f. _____

g. _____

h. _____

5.3.4   Write down the discussion questions or topics you will use to draw out inferences from the students themselves about the *relevance* (to them *personally*) of the enabling objective or subtask that has been identified.

_____

_____

_____

_____

5.3.5   Referring to Activity 5.3.3, organize the major topics into an outline to which you can refer during the discussion.

For example: I.   Introduction
                           A.   Major point
                                   1. Illustrations, examples

                        II.   Discussion questions

Describe when each activity will occur and what you and the students will be doing. Write this on a separate sheet and attach here.

Now there is a basic structure to the discussion you are planning. In order to keep the discussion on the track, it is a good idea to communicate the general outline to the students and to periodically review how much of the outline has been discussed. Instructors have various ways of doing this: writing key words or a brief outline on the board; writing study questions on the board or on handout sheets (with room for students' responses); or having students design questions that may be rephrased for the group, among others.

Such a structure does not imply inflexibility. Students may still bring relevant examples and experiences into the discussion, and may pursue a line of discussion beyond its preplanned limits. That's fine—as long as the time is constructively spent and all participants have an opportunity to take part. The function of the written outline is to keep the discussion relatively on track, to remind the discussion leader and participants when they are going into a territory that has little relevance for the major points of the discussion. Sometimes digression begins to develop into a constructive discussion on a different topic. Good teachers who recognize this will, from time to time, set aside their original plans and move with an animated discussion that may serve other acceptable objectives. For the time being, let's plan a method for informing discussion participants of the major topics to be covered.

5.3.6 Describe how you will communicate the outline of the discussion to the participants (attach copies of handouts or other materials you plan to use for this purpose).

_____

_____

_____

_____

5.3.7 List any instructions you will give at the beginning of the discussion (such as rules of order, boundaries of the topic, or how long each person may speak at a time).

_____

_____

_____

_____

5.3.8 **a.** Write down in detail the introductory statement you will use to initiate the discussion and direct its course. If you will use a short film or reading, indicate exactly how you will introduce it.

_____

_____

_____

_____

_____

b. Will you use any examples to support your introductory point? Write down what they will be.

_____

_____

_____

_____

_____

c. Write down three specific comments you could make to draw attention to the important aspects of your examples. These may be in the form of questions.

1. _____

2. _____

3. _____

5.3.9 How will you provide for active and relevant student responding?

a. What forms of responding are most appropriate to the practice of the desired terminal behavior (critical comments, analytical questions, personal opinions, answers to others' queries)? Provide three specific examples of appropriate responses.

1. _____

_____

2. _____

_____

3. _____

_____

b. List three to five specific signals to initiate responses from individual students.

1. _____

2. _____

3. _____

4. _____

5. _____

5.3.10 What will you do and say if one or two students tend to dominate the discussion? Refer to Activity 4 for ideas on reducing disruptive behaviors in a positive manner. Avoid negative statements—"You talk too much"—and sarcastic comments. Use *positive*, nonoffensive procedures.

_____

_____

_____

_____

5.3.11 a. Write down three prompting comments you will make if the discussion seems to drag or if the students appear confused.

1. _____

_____

2. _____

_____

3. _____

_____

    b. What other procedures will you use if the discussion slows down or the conversation wanders from the topic? Describe two of them specifically.

       1. _____

          _____

       2. _____

          _____

5.3.12 How will students receive and use informational feedback?

    a. List three forms of feedback you will use if you lead the discussion. Give a specific illustration of the use of each in your discussion lesson.

       1. _____

       2. _____

       3. _____

    b. Suggest how the results (feedback) should be used by the students. (Should they contemplate, ask another question, revise and restate the comment?)

          _____

          _____

          _____

Occasionally, in an extended discussion, it makes sense for the discussion leader to stop and summarize—or ask a student to summarize—the major points that have been covered and the conclusions reached. Such intermittent summing up accomplishes several things. It provides a review, facilitating learning; it allows the students to fill in points they may have missed, and to complete more detailed notes; and it serves as a reinforcer— "See how much we have accomplished."

5.3.13 **a.** Can you think of any other purposes that might be served by a periodic summing up?

_____

_____

_____

b. At what points in the discussion and *how,* specifically, do you plan to sum up? _____

_____

c. Describe exactly how you plan to summarize the outcomes of the discussion. _____

_____

_____

_____

5.3.14 Now go over the outline you prepared for Activity 5.3.5 and, on a new sheet of paper, integrate Activities 5.3.6–5.3.13 into a full procedural outline. Bring to class this outline plus any materials (especially any you prepared yourself) that will be used for the discussion.

You are now ready to hold your discussion. With such careful planning, it is bound to be a success. Good luck and have fun!

5.3.15 Write any relevant comments on or suggestions for Activity 5 and Format 5.3.

_____

_____

_____

FORMAT 5.4

LABORATORY FORMAT (PROBLEM-SOLVING FORMAT)

Problem-solving activities range along a very broad continuum from highly structured forms—"make a .003 titration of sodium hydroxide"—to those for which a great deal of original thought is required—"We are going to plan a trip to Mars: Sue's group is in charge of life systems, Mark's group will plan the on-site experiments." This latter type of activity is very similar to artistic expression—the student must evaluate his or her own knowledge of the world as it relates to the problem at hand (application), and bring that knowledge together (synthesis) to create a solution, using the resources provided. It is not coincidental that we speak metaphorically of "molding ideas." Problem-solving formats allow the student a special sort of independence. A student can choose those ideas or resources he or she knows best and work with them in depth. The amount of independence the student has depends, of course, upon the specification of the desired result of the activity, and upon the variety of resources provided.

5.4.1 Choose an enabling objective or subtask with which you feel thoroughly familiar. Write it down in a final form.

_____

_____

_____

5.4.2 **a.** List the specific goals of this laboratory session.

_____

_____

_____

_____

_____

b. Write down a description of the criteria you will provide for your students so they will know exactly what type of finished product or solution you expect.

_____

_____

_____

_____

5.4.3 List any additional instructions necessary for the students at the beginning of the lesson. Include specific directions as to the approach or "type of thinking" they should use in the lab—critical, creative, "hard facts," or imaginative.

_____

_____

_____

_____

5.4.4 How will your students participate in the lab and in what form will they present their solution or product?

a. What forms of response are most appropriate as practice for the desired terminal behavior (answering questions, performing skills, giving individual presentations)? Give specific examples below.

_____

_____

_____

_____

_____

b. List five appropriate signals to initiate the response.

1. _____

2 _____

3. _____

4. _____

5. _____

c. In the event that students are unable to make the desired response, list three ways you will prompt them. Include a sample of each. (Consider such possibilities as workbooks, sample solutions, and "first step" guidance.)

1. _____

2. _____

3. _____

d. Specify the conditions (as defined in your objective) for appropriate practice. (Will the students use books or lists of formulas, can they confer with classmates, is there a time limit on response production?)

_____

_____

_____

_____

_____

5.4.5   How will students receive and use informative feedback?

a.   List three forms of feedback you will employ during the instruction and give an illustration of each, derived from your lesson. (Teacher answers, exchanges of papers for immediate grading, checking own answers against text, or posting of expected results are some possibilities.) Indicate when the feedback will occur relative to the response.

1. _____

_____

2. _____

_____

3. _____

_____

b.   Suggest how the feedback will be used by the students. (Will they redesign the experiments, take a second mastery quiz, explain the idea more fully to classmates?)

_____

_____

_____

Organize all the procedures you have described into an orderly sequence. List the sequence of your procedures in outline form. (Indicate when the students will be doing what; where the response and feedback sequences will occur; what the teacher will be doing; when and how each presentation or explanation will be given; and approximately how much time is planned for each of these stages.) Activity 5.1.3 (in the General Format 5.1) contains a brief example of such an outline; you may wish to review this example before making your own outline.

5.4.6 Now write your instructional sequence. (Please print or type. Feel free to use as many pages as necessary.)

5.4.7 Provide yourself with all the necessary materials for questions you will be asking, descriptions you will give, or demonstrations you will perform. List possible questions and the desired responses; write brief descriptions of any special steps in your procedure; then organize all your materials according to your outline.

_____

_____

_____

_____

_____

_____

_____

_____

5.4.8 **a.** Have all the properties described in the "Designing an Instructional Sequence" section of Activity 5 been used in your outline? Yes _____ No _____

b. If any procedure has been omitted, decide where it should go or justify its exclusion.

_____

_____

_____

_____

5.4.9 Check your materials and outline against these criteria.

    a. Is the lesson sequenced properly? _____

    b. Are your *instructional stimuli* likely to be effective and appropriate? _____ Do they occasion responses appropriate to the student's behavioral repertoire? _____

    c. Have you specified precisely the *materials* you will use? _____

    d. Have you keyed your instruction to the *interests and aspirations* of your students? _____

    e. Have you provided for *active* response by the students? _____

    f. Have you enlisted several forms of *informative feedback* (at least two)? _____

    g. Is the feedback provided
        frequently? _____
        with minimal delay? _____
        consistently? _____
        often as an appropriate response following the student response? _____

    h. Is progress toward the objective *reinforced* along the way? _____

5.4.10 Write your comments on and suggestions for Activity 5 and Format 5.4.

_____

_____

_____

_____

FORMAT 5.5

ON-SITE FORMAT

Games, field trips, simulations, and role playing are all formats in which students can learn concepts, skills, and behaviors in the settings where they apply, or in facsimiles of those settings. Such designs, in addition to using high-level cognitive skills, are inherently exciting. The relevance of enabling objectives or subtasks is often self-evident in realistic situations. Because such experiences have so many different facets, the information they yield can motivate students to engage in various related educational activities, such as themes, art work, displays, plays, or debates.

5.5.1   Write down the enabling objective or subtask(s) for which you are designing your on-site format.

_____

_____

_____

5.5.2   List the specific goals of this experience.

_____

_____

_____

5.5.3   How will environmental stimuli be arranged and used?

a.   What type of setting is appropriate for the application of the concepts, skills, and behaviors to be taught?

_____

_____

_____

b. Will you use a real situation or a simulated one? If you have a choice, what are the advantages of each?

_____

_____

_____

_____

c. What are the logistics of the situation? Include considerations of cost, safety, school-board policy, parent permission, time, transportation, and space.

_____

_____

_____

_____

_____

_____

d. Will you require the assistance of outside personnel or props? Describe exactly what they will be and how you will obtain them.

_____

_____

_____

_____

_____

e. Decide whether you or the students (or someone else) will design the rules or instructions for the experience. List the rules or instructions if you are going to provide them yourself, or describe how you will instruct the students and guide them in designing their own.

_____

_____

_____

_____

5.5.4 How will you provide for active and relevant student responding?

a. What forms of response will be practiced in this situation? List several examples and indicate how they are appropriate to the desired terminal behavior.

_____

_____

_____

_____

_____

b. List five appropriate signals to initiate student responses.

1. _____

2. _____

3. _____

4. _____

5. _____

c. How and by whom will the signals to initiate these responses be provided?

_____

_____

d. What kinds of prompts, if any, would be appropriate in this situation? Describe three.

1. _____

2. _____

3. _____

e. Specify the conditions for appropriate practice, as defined in your instructional objective (Activity 1.19). (Will students have lists of actions to choose from? Will they be provided with scripts, and should these be memorized? Can classmates direct a student's actions?)

_____

_____

_____

_____

5.5.5 How will students receive and use informative feedback?

a. Does the activity provide its own feedback? Where? How often?

_____

_____

b. Will fellow students or the teacher comment on performance? Yes _____ No _____

c. Indicate when the feedback will occur relative to the response (upon the return home, during the performance or game, following each role sequence).

_____

_____

_____

d. Suggest how the results of feedback will be used by the student. (Will the game be played a second time, will the student write an evaluation of his or her role?)

_____

_____

_____

5.5.6 Outline, on separate sheets of paper, how the game, simulation, or field trip will be organized. List an appropriate sequence of events; indicate how it will begin and end; and indicate whether all students should be involved, and what each should be doing. For a field trip, for example, you should indicate whether you will stay together as a group or break up and pursue different activities at different times. Include time elements (how long to read the script or memorize it, how long the episode will last).

5.5.7 Provide yourself with all the necessary materials for the experience (game board or props, scripts, role descriptions) and organize these materials according to your outline.

5.5.8 Make sure you have included the four properties described in the introduction to Activity 5. If one is not included, revise the outline to incorporate all four properties, or explain why a property has been excluded.

_____

_____

5.5.9 Check your materials and outline against these criteria.

    a. Is the lesson *sequenced* properly? _____

    b. Are your *instructional stimuli* likely to be effective and appropriate? _____ Do they occasion responses appropriate to the student's behavioral repertoire? _____

    c. Have you specified precisely the *materials* you will use? _____

    d. Have you keyed your instruction to the *interests and aspirations* of your students? _____

    e. Have you provided for *active* response by the student? _____

    f. Have you enlisted several forms of *informative* feedback (at least two)? _____

    g. Is the feedback provided
        frequently? _____
        with minimal delay? _____
        consistently? _____
        often as an appropriate response following the student response? _____

    h. Is progress toward the objective *reinforced* along the way? _____

5.5.10 Write your comments on and suggestions for Activity 5 and Format 5.5.

_____

_____

_____

_____

_____

FORMAT 5.6

STUDENT-DESIGNED FORMAT

Allowing students to choose their own format and design their own learning procedure is often desirable. It can enhance interest in the learning experience by giving them a voice in selecting the most appropriate and relevant forms of practice, and by reinforcing them personally. Many teachers find the prospect of giving such freedom to students rather frightening, but it needn't be if procedures are properly organized in advance.

The main consideration is: How *much* freedom are you willing to let the students have? Are you willing to let them write their own objectives from scratch and design procedures for achieving them, or does the curriculum under which you are teaching require that you specify the goals, or even the precise instructional objectives, yourself? May the students choose *any* format they wish, or will you offer a specific set of alternatives?

It is you who must set the limits within which your students will operate. Be honest with yourself when you are setting these limits. If you cannot operate efficiently in some formats, do not include those formats among the alternatives you make available to your students. Every teacher has talents *and* limitations—*know yours*.

Once you have decided where *your* limits lie, you must do the same for your students. Quite possibly your students have never before been offered the chance to make educational decisions for themselves. If you wish to have them design their own lessons "from the ground up," you may need to lead them to it gradually. They will probably have no more idea of how to organize their lessons than you did when you first began. At first, you will probably want to suggest alternatives for them to choose from and do most of the planning yourself. As they become more familiar with these alternatives, your students will be able to accept greater and greater responsibility for the design of their lessons.

Many of the questions in the preceding formats are directed toward the teacher. If you wish to have a wholly or partially student-designed format, you will not be making some of these decisions. In that case, what *you* need to provide is a set of instructions for the students, clarifying or listing any limits or restrictions of the format. Maybe you will want to design a format like ours, filling in the appropriate sections yourself to help your students get organized. Whatever you choose to do, remember that your students will need *more* assistance and guidance, not less, as they learn to use their new-found educational freedom.

One method you might consider to provide some structure is the *contracting system.* The contract—as a business contract does—specifies what each party will do within what time limit, and what will be gained by each in return. For instance, a music student might want to independently learn more about electronic music. This student proposes listening to and evaluating a specified number of records or tapes; writing a three-page report on the history of electronic music; and preparing an electronic-music tape to present to the class along with a brief accompanying lecture by a given date. In return, the teacher agrees that satisfactory completion of these activities will earn the student one-third of the semester grade. This agreement is written, signed by both parties (and a witness, if they desire), and filed for future reference.

5.6.1 Write your comments or suggestions on Activity 5 and Format 5.6.

_____

_____

_____

_____

_____

_____

_____

_____

_____

_____

_____

_____

SUPPLEMENTARY EXERCISES

1. School Observation to Aid Your Preparation of Instructional Materials and Procedures

Purpose: To enable you to observe active instruction in operation.

Arrange with your instructor to visit a school that has a group similar to the one you are currently (or hope one day to be) teaching. Observe the group for several hours. Note the following information:

1. the purpose of the instructional activity

2. the materials available to students and to the teacher

3. a brief description of the students themselves

4. a brief description of the teacher and his or her background

5. the activities in which the students are engaging

6. the activities in which the teacher or supervisor is engaging

7. a description of any permanent products produced by the students—for example, papers or art objects (attach samples if possible)

8. a description of any form of assessment used to evaluate student accomplishment

9. any records that are kept by the teacher or students to chart progress

10. a description of the students' apparent interest or motivation vis-a-vis the activities

11. your general impression of the instructional activities

12. your comments or suggestions.

2. Teacher Interview

Purpose: To allow you to participate in an instructional evaluation and review process.

1. Arrange an interview with a teacher. If you have completed Supplementary Exercise 1, try to arrange a meeting with the teacher you observed for that exercise. If not, arrange a meeting with any teacher who is working with a group of interest to you.

2. Discuss with the teacher the items covered in the previous exercise; however, this time ask the teacher to give his or her impressions of the effectiveness of the instructional sequencing, and any changes that he or she might make the next time the activities in the sequence are conducted.

3. Locating Instructional Resource Materials

Purpose: To provide you with additional sources for designing your instructional sequence. You should give your instructor notes, note cards, or an outline based on one or more of the following resources:

1. Go to a curriculum library in a local school system and look through the teachers' editions of textbooks.

2. Ask a friend who is currently teaching to allow you to look through his or her instructional materials.

3. Visit your university or public library and look for ideas in the education

section, or in sections that have materials for children and youth.

4. Visit a self-instruction center in a university and look through some of the programmed instructional material.

5. Look through textbooks that are used in methods or curriculum-development courses at the university level.

6. Check with your instructor, or consult the phone book, to find out if there are any special-education materials centers in your region. Such centers are distributed throughout the country. Go to one of these centers and look at some of the in-

structional materials used for students with special needs.

7. Set up an interview (with the help of your instructor) with an individual teaching at a local state institution or training facility for special populations. Discuss and look through the instructional material being used.

8. Check with your instructor to see if there is a film library or audio-visual materials center on your campus. If so, look through the catalog of films and other audio-visual material, particularly through the curriculum materials.

SUGGESTED READINGS AND REFERENCES

Anastasiow, N. *Educational Psychology: A Contemporary View.* Del Mar, Ca.: Communications Research Machines, 1973. Chapter 11, pp. 207–27 (development of instructional methods).

Anderson, R. C., and Faust, G. W. *Educational Psychology: The Science of Instruction and Learning.* New York: Dodd, Mead & Co., 1973. Introduction to chapter 6, pp. 187–92 (a model of teaching).

Bushell, D., Jr. *Classroom Behavior.* Englewood Cliffs, N.J.: Prentice-Hall, 1974. Chapter 3, pp. 36–37 (instructional sequence).

DeCecco, J. P., and Crawford, W. R. *The Psychology of Learning and Instruction.* Englewood Cliffs, N.J.: Prentice-Hall, 1974. Chapter 1, pp. 8–22 (instructional procedures and models).

Gagné, R. M. *Essentials of Learning for Instruction.* Hinsdale, Ill.: The Dryden Press, 1974. Chapter 5, pp. 97–122 (instructional procedures).

Givner, A., and Graubard, P. S. *A Handbook of Behavior Modification for the Classroom.* New York: Holt, Rinehart & Winston, 1974. Chapter 5, pp. 132–35 (developing specific teaching strategies).

Klausmeier, H. J., and Goodwin, W. *Learning and Human Abilities: Educational Psychology.* 4th ed. New York: Harper & Row, Publishers, 1966. Chapter 1, pp. 4–9 (instructional programming for the individual student).

Lefrancois, G. R. *Psychology for Teaching.* Belmont, Ca.: Wadsworth Publishing Co., 1975. Chapter 1, pp. 8–10 (teaching models and instructional strategy).

Smith, M. D. *Educational Psychology and Its Classroom Applications.* Boston: Allyn & Bacon, 1975. Chapter 14, pp. 403–26 (examples of instructional systems, old and new); chapter 15, pp. 427–69 (development of instructional systems).

For Format 5.1:

Anderson, R. C., and Faust, G. W. *Educational Psychology: The Science of Instruction and Learning.* New York: Dodd, Mead & Co., 1973. Chapter 1, pp. 22–41 (examples of programmed instruction); chapter 10, pp. 346–65.

Becker, W. C.; Englemann, S.; and Thomas, D. R. *Teaching 1: Classroom Management.* Chicago:

Science Research Associates, 1975. Unit 12, pp. 240–45 (contracting).

Biehler, R. F. *Psychology Applied to Teaching.* Boston: Houghton Mifflin Co., 1971. Chapter 6, pp. 229–47 (problem solving); chapter 5, pp. 169–72 (programmed learning and the teacher, writing your own program, and using published programs); chapter 15, pp. 528–31 (lecture or discussion?).

Blair, G. M.; Jones, R. S.; and Simpson, R. H. *Educational Psychology.* New York: Macmillan Co., 1975. Chapter 9, pp. 248–54 (problem solving).

DeCecco, J. P., and Crawford, W. R. *The Psychology of Learning and Instruction.* Englewood Cliffs, N.J.: Prentice-Hall, 1974. Chapter 11, pp. 324–43 (problem solving and instruction for problem solving); chapter 12, pp. 369–90 (programmed instruction).

Gagné, R. M. *Essentials of Learning for Instruction.* Hinsdale, Ill.: The Dryden Press, 1974. Chapter 6, pp. 128–30 (problem solving), and pp. 134–35 (self-instruction).

Givner, A., and Graubard, P. S. *A Handbook of Behavior Modification for the Classroom.* New York: Holt, Rinehart & Winston, 1974. Chapter 5, pp. 135–43 (programmed material).

Klausmeier, H. J., and Goodwin, W. *Learning and Human Abilities: Educational Psychology.* 4th ed. New York: Harper & Row, Publishers, 1966. Chapter 5, pp. 121–29 (programmed instructional material); chapter 12, pp. 300–308 and pp. 313–21 (problem solving).

Lefrancois, G. R. *Psychology for Teaching.* Belmont, Ca.: Wadsworth Publishing Co., 1975. Chapter 4, pp. 67–84 (programmed learning).

Meacham, M. L., and Wiesen, A. E. *Changing Classroom Behavior.* 2nd ed. New York: Intext Educational Publishers, 1974. Part 1, chapter 7, pp. 105–10 (programmed instruction and programming).

Smith, M. D. *Educational Psychology and Its Classroom Applications.* Boston: Allyn & Bacon, 1975. Chapter 11, pp. 306–19 (problem solving); chapter 13, pp. 381–400 (components and media for instructional systems—includes lectures, demonstration, programmed instruction, games and simulation, and student-designed formats).

Sulzer, B., and Mayer, G. R. *Behavior Modification Procedures for School Personnel.* Hinsdale, Ill.: The Dryden Press, 1972. Chapter 4, pp. 72–75 (programmed instruction).

Taber, J. I.; Glaser, R.; and Schaefer, H. H. *Learning and Programmed Instruction.* Reading, Mass.: Addison-Wesley Publishing Co., 1965. Chapters 4–7, pp. 62–150 (programmed instruction); chapter 8, pp. 151–74 (examples of the use of programmed instruction).

For Format 5.2:

Markle, S. M. *Good Frames and Bad: A Grammar of Frame Writing.* New York: Wiley, 1969.

Taber, J. K.; Glaser, R.; and Schafer, H. H. *Learning and Programmed Instruction.* Reading, Mass.: Addison-Wesley Publishing Co., 1965.

Illustrative Programs

Anderson, R. C., and Faust, G. W. *Educational Psychology.* New York: Dodd, Mead & Co., 1973. Pp. 21–41. The authors illustrate programmed instruction in their section on instructional objectives.

Buchanan, C. D., ed. *Sullivan Associates Program.* New York: McGraw-Hill, 1965. A programmed reading series and a programmed math series for elementary-school children.

Hendershot, C. H., ed. *Programmed Learning and Individually Paced Instruction—Bibliography.* 5th ed. n.p., 1974.

Holland, J., and Skinner, B. F. *The Analysis of Behavior: A Program for Self-Instruction.* New York: McGraw-Hill, 1961.

Mager, R. F. *Preparing Instructional Objectives for Programmed Instruction.* San Francisco: Fearon Publishers, 1962.

Skinner, B. F., and Krackower, S.A. *Handwriting with Write and See.* Chicago: Lyons & Carnahan, 1968. For elementary-school children.

6

EVALUATION, REVISION, AND IMPLEMENTATION

Objectives

When you have completed this activity, you should be able to:

- write an enabling objective or subtask as you plan to teach it, including a complete statement of methods for assessing its accomplishment

- design an evaluation system with items measuring:
  entering behaviors
  behaviors required to accomplish your enabling objective or subtask
  progress and task completion
  terminal behaviors (as specified in your instructional objective)
  delayed retention incorporating the properties of validity, reliability, and objectivity

- construct answer keys or criteria checklists that can be used independently by another staff member or by the students themselves

- administer the lesson and evaluation as designed

- obtain feedback from students and supervisors

- modify your lesson plan in accordance with the results of your instruction and evaluation

Evaluation, Revision, and Implementation

You have just about everything ready now to carry out the instruction you have so carefully planned. Your enabling objective or subtask has been completely expanded into a full set of materials and procedures; everything is in order. At this point you are probably anxious to implement your plan. But wait! There is one more aspect of instructional design that requires consideration: an evaluation plan—and making whatever revisions in your instructional design are indicated by your evaluation. When this is accomplished you should have an end product that will reward your efforts.

Continuous evaluation is an essential aspect of the instructional model we are presenting here. Evaluation is woven into its whole methodology—before, during, and after instruction. Post-instruction evaluation may involve "proving" to yourself or to others that you've done a good job, but that is only one of its functions. Grades, of course, are required in some form by most school systems, and these will have to conform to school policy. The main purpose of your teaching, however, is to enable your students to achieve educational goals—that is, to enable students to acquire the behaviors specified by your instructional objectives. A proper evaluation method is designed to assess such acquisition while it is in progress and afterwards, rather than to serve primarily as the basis for grades. Evaluations should measure objectively the learning that is occurring at present and that has taken place already in your classroom.

In this activity you are going to be asked to design and implement several types of evaluation: an assessment of the entering behaviors that you identified for Activity 3, so you can determine if your students are ready to profit from your planned instruction; a review and possible refinement of the methods that you identified in Activity 4.1 for assessing the completion of subtasks, to allow you to check student progress and to adjust instruction if necessary; a posttest evaluation, to assess how well the objectives or task behaviors have been acquired; and an optional delayed-retention test, to determine if the new learning has persisted.

A beneficial byproduct of a behaviorally-based evaluation system is the objective information it produces. When objective criteria are applied to student performance, grading becomes more valid and reliable. Any mystery surrounding the assignment of grades can finally be solved simply by telling your students exactly the criteria upon which their performances will be evaluated. You can specify grading procedures on the first day of class. Your students, realizing that the system is fair and reasonable, will concentrate on learning rather than on "beating the system."

The same unbiased, specific information provides a ready means of communication with your supervisors (as well as with parents and other interested people). You can describe the objectives, your instructional procedures, and the outcome of instruction for each student. Consider the effect of presenting your supervisor with the empirical evidence that twenty-seven of your twenty-eight students have met the instructional objective of being "able to spell correctly at least twenty-three of twenty-five words drawn from the new word list in their current readers," instead of having to say that "most of them are pretty good spellers." If your evaluation procedure is thorough, you will also be able to describe the remedial instruction you prescribed for the one student who didn't meet the criterion, assuring that all students will eventually achieve the objective. As a result of your specific teaching practices, the supervisor will know precisely what you and your students have accomplished—a highly rewarding state of affairs.

Now for the procedures involved in behaviorally-based evaluation. At the beginning, you must designate exactly what the performances are that you wish to evaluate. This part is simple, since the instructional objectives you have already written indicate the appropriate performances, conditions, and criteria of performance.

6.1   Write the instructional objective you've chosen and the enabling objective, subtask, or series of subtasks you've developed into an instructional sequence.

Instructional objective: _____

_____

_____

Enabling objective or subtask: _____

_____

_____

_____

In many cases a test is an appropriate assessment instrument. If you use a test, remember that you should be testing to assess mastery of the specific enabling objective or subtask you have taught rather than to "separate the good students from the bad." If you keep this in mind, your questions will be written differently. You are not trying to write "hard" questions, but rather test items that will accurately indicate your students' degree of acquisition of the enabling objective or subtask. There are three important criteria for any evaluation procedure—validity, reliability, and objectivity.

Validity
A test is valid if it actually measures what it is intended to measure. The use of behavioral objectives makes validity easy to test—you simply ask whether your evaluation items measure the performance as specified in your objectives. If you can accurately assess from test results the students' ability to perform the enabling objective or subtask, your test is valid. Some suggestions for enhancing validity follow.

- Don't give "hints" on your exam or in the question that might give away the correct answer.

- State your questions clearly to avoid misleading or confusing the learner. In general, avoid negative statements in your questions, or if you use them emphasize the negator so it can't be missed.

- Select items that are different from examples used in class.

Reliability

A reliable test will give the same or consistent results for equivalent performances. Equal performances will result in equal scores, or two administrations of the test to the same person (providing this student learns nothing extra between the exams) will result in comparable scores.

- Reliability can be increased by using scoring keys for exams to aid in consistent judgment.

- When performances are graded on some qualitative level, try to convert the grading to a checklist that the scorer can use to mark specific occurrences of desired behaviors.

Objectivity

Biases about individual students, the desire to have all assigned grades be high, the order of papers during grading, and your own condition at the moment you are assigning grades can seriously affect the fairness of your decisions. Objective assessment requires total reliance on the actual empirical evidence presented during evaluation.

- The procedures useful for increasing reliability tend to make scoring more specific and performance-oriented—and therefore more objective.

- Other procedures include blind scoring (replacing students' names on papers with numbers or codes); having several judges grade each paper; or handing out answer sheets and allowing students to attempt to justify answers marked as incorrect.

Assessing Cognitive, Psychomotor, and Affective Objectives

Cognitive objectives are assessed in many ways. Most students are already familiar with paper-and-pencil tests, laboratory mock-ups, problem-solving situations, and assignments requiring the application of certain knowledge.

The more clearly the objective is written, the more apparent it is what kind of "test" would be appropriate. Consider this instructional objective: "Given twenty specimens of rock, the student should be able to differentiate the igneous from the sedimentary, making no more than two incorrect identifications." Selecting a method to assess this objective is relatively straightforward—a checklist or written laboratory sheet would be sufficient.

Many of the objectives of formal instructional programs, such as comprehension and simple "knowledge" items, are more fundamental. When it is apparent that the most valid means for assessing such objectives is through paper-and-pencil tests of the short-answer variety, the following considerations and practice may be helpful to the instructional planner.

Is the test clearly related to your objective(s)? The "score," when obtained, should mean something to you. If it is just a number, you have missed the point. While it is all right to combine two or more objectives in one item, you should have some means of checking *which* objectives have or have not been met. Be certain this is possible.

Is the test practical? Consider all the possible logistical problems. Is your test short enough for the time allotted and the interest span of your students? Is it standardized and keyed so that someone could administer it if you were not there? Is it comprehensible, and interesting or provocative for the students? Does it require any special facilities? Have you allowed sufficient space for the types and "amounts" of responses desired?

If you're looking for a more open-ended, flexible system of evaluation, alternatives are available. As we discussed in Activity 1.18, a list of characteristics may be generated for complex behaviors and for constructed responses or performances (essays, sculptures, plays, speeches, diving, or gymnastics). These may then be arranged to form a checklist.

Many behaviors better evaluated by observation than by paper-and-pencil tests lend themselves to the use of a checklist. Swimming and other psychomotor behaviors are easily evaluated by a checklist. In fact, the subtasks you choose for your record-keeping system may be the only checklist you need, or you may want to elaborate upon your system for only certain tasks. A step such as "gets into the water" stands alone, while "swims a length of the pool" can have subitems on the checklist such as "turns head to breathe," and "moves arms correctly." Often the subitems will turn out to be entering or enabling behaviors.

Look over the steps you chose to use in your record-keeping system and consider whether they would form an appropriate basis for a checklist. If you wish, use one step for all or part of your evaluation system. Another way to construct a checklist is to write some checklist items instead of test questions as responses to the exercises that follow.

Assessment of affective objectives may be accomplished in several ways. Probably the most valid is a behavioral-choice system. Several choices are offered; the student selects one. This choice would indicate preference for a particular task. For example, presume that one subobjective of a swimming program is that the student enjoy swimming. Various alternatives—a soccer game, free play, or swimming class—could be made available. The student's selection of swimming over the other two activities would provide a direct behavioral assessment of the student's preference for swimming.

Paper-and-pencil tests may also be used as indirect measures of some affective objectives. Many such tests have been devised, including one that asks direct questions about the activity—for example, "Rate your preference for this activity. Given a choice between the first activity and the second activity, which would you choose? To which activity would you like to bring a friend?"

Remembering that you can use tests or checklists, combine aspects of each, or prepare some other method, adapt these instructions for writing tests to your own needs. Feel free to use any other method you can devise if you find it more appropriate. These instructions are intended to serve as general but flexible guidelines, not rigid requirements. Whatever you choose to do, compare your evaluation procedure to the evaluation procedure checklist provided.

6.2   If you are working with a cognitive enabling objective or subtask, complete the following:*

Objective Items

- *Be clear about the factors that determine the correctness of the response ahead of time, not after the fact.* Choose one of your subtasks and check it to be certain you have specified exactly what constitutes a correct or an incorrect response.

a.   Specify the correct response in the space provided below.

Correct response: _____

- *State the question as clearly and precisely as possible.* Check the items with several other people to be certain they are understandable.

---

*These suggestions for writing tests were abstracted and adapted primarily from Robert L. Thorndike, *Educational Measurement*, 2nd ed. (Washington, D.C.: American Council on Education, 1971).

b. Indicate which of the following two questions is stated more precisely.

1. If a person were doing nothing in particular and we decided to record some of his brain waves, we might attach some electrodes and record:
   a. beta waves
   b. alpha waves
   c. electrowaves

2. The brain waves recorded by an electroencephalograph during quiet wakefulness when the brain is "at rest" are called:
   a. beta waves
   b. alpha waves
   c. electrowaves

c. Choose one of your subtasks. After attempting several versions on scratch paper, write a clear, precise question to assess its attainment. (You may wish to use this question in completing Activities 6.3–6.8.)

_____

_____

_____

- *State items positively or underline the negative terms.*

d. Rewrite the following question in a positive form.
Although it is true that American presidents have come from many "walks of life," from which groups have they not come?

_____

_____

_____

- *Test questions should require responses that use only those skills that are relevant to the instructional objective, or those known to be in the student's repertoire.*

e. Check your answer for question 2b against your analysis of entering behaviors in Activity 3. Have you required any new behaviors not related to the objective? If so, rewrite the question below to eliminate such irrelevant sources of difficulty. (Feel free to reuse this item for Activities 6.3–6.8.)

_____

_____

_____

• *Avoid irrelevant clues unless you specifically intend to prompt the student response.* The most common form of overprompting is grammatical cueing.

f. Circle the question below which illustrates grammatical overprompting.

   1. What is the best synonym for "frolicking"?
     a. to run
     b. playing
     c. work
     d. frightened

   2. What is the best synonym for "climate"?
     a. weather
     b. rain
     c. quality
     d. summit

• *Avoid stereotyped phraseology (such as repetition of complex phrases) that enables response-by-rote, unless the goal is memorization.*

g. Rewrite the following two questions to test for a higher level of cognitive skill (refer to Activity 2 if you wish to review Bloom's classifications).

   1. The two major American parties in recent history have been the Republicans and the _____.

2. Every proper sentence includes a subject, an object, and a:
   a. word
   b. period
   c. clause
   d. verb

Multiple-Choice Items

- *Responses should be arranged in logical order, but the position of the correct response should vary from item to item.*

h. Choose the item with the more appropriate arrangement of responses.

1. How many inches are there in a foot?
   a. 3
   b. 5
   c. 10
   d. 12

2. In what year did the United States declare its independence?
   a. 1974
   b. 1812
   c. 1776
   d. 1779

- *Make distractors plausible and attractive, especially to those students with common misconceptions or who make common errors.* Use "none of these" only if an absolutely correct answer is possible or if all the distractors are definitely rejectable.

i. Choose the item which has the more plausible distractors.

1. Psychology is the study of:
   a. crazy people
   b. books
   c. behavior
   d. monkeys

2. Psychology is the study of:
   a. thoughts
   b. behavior
   c. experimental data
   d. abnormal behavior

- *Distractors should also incorporate the knowledge gained by the student as part of the task or knowledge already in the student's repertoire.* They should be no more difficult to reject than the correct answer is to accept.

j. From the list provided, select four good distractors for the following question.

1. Another word for "affective" is:

    a. _____   eustatic
                                 emotional
    b. _____   important
                                 spurious
    c. _____   effective
                                 reflective
    d. _____   loving
                                 afferent

k. Refer to your task analysis and write a multiple-choice item for one of your subtasks. Be sure the distractors can be rejected on the basis of skills included in that analysis. (This item may be used again in response to Activities 6.3–6.8.)

_____

_____

_____

_____

Constructed-Response Items

Fill-Ins

Fill-ins are appropriate only for questions answerable in a unique word, phrase, or symbol. They should be used only for practice in using a particular word or phrase to be memorized, such as a formula or technical term.

For example: "The style of painting originated by Seurat is referred to specifically as _____."

1. If you have an enabling objective or subtask that requires memorization of a term, phrase, or symbol, write an appropriate fill-in item below. (You may use this response to complete Activities 6.3–6.8.)

_____

_____

Short Answers

Make the question explicit so students can tell if they've "said enough." Provide cues about the criteria. For example, if the question is computational, specify the degree of precision required. Here is an example:

Describe in a few sentences how the neural impulse is transmitted along a neuron. Be sure to include discussion of the initiation process, chemical changes that take place, and any terminating processes that may exist. (6 points)

m. Now write a short-answer question for one of your subtasks. Be certain to include appropriate cues. (You may use this for Activities 6.3–6.8.)

_____

_____

_____

_____

6.3 Design at least five items to evaluate the entering behaviors you have listed for the enabling objective, subtask, or series of subtasks you chose to work with in Activity 3. These do not need to be standard-form questions, but can include any procedures appropriate to the assessment of relevant behaviors. If you plan on oral questioning, write an outline and at least one complete question you will ask for each topic. These will be used for preassessment. Write or describe the items on a separate sheet of paper.

6.4 Describe the system you will use to assess completion of each of the subtasks that constitute your instructional sequence. Will you use the record you designed for Activity 4.2? Do you think it would be appropriate to modify your record? If so, describe your modifications:

_____

_____

_____

6.5 Write (on separate sheets of paper) at least one posttest or evaluation item for each subtask behavior that you are planning to teach. Employ at least four different types of formats (multiple choice, true/false, fill-ins, short constructed responses, matching), if applicable.

6.6 Even though you may not be planning to teach a full instructional objective, write (on separate sheets of paper) approximately four evaluation items or procedures for your instructional objective. Try to use different forms of communication, and different modes of student responding: written, oral, audio-visual, and motor. If you are using fill-ins or multiple-choice, you may need many more than four items to cover your objective.

6.7 Choose representative items from 6.5 and 6.6 (at least two from each) and rewrite them for use in your preassessment procedure.

_____

_____

_____

_____

_____

_____

6.8   Organize items from 6.3 and 6.7 into a short preassessment procedure. Construct a grading key or checklist for it.

6.9   Using the items you designed in 6.5 and 6.6, organize a complete postevaluation to conduct following instruction. Include all the items for relevant entering behaviors and enabling objectives. Hint: research tentatively indicates that student response is better when simpler items come at the beginning of the evaluation procedure.

6.10   Write a complete scoring key for use with the exam or procedure you constructed in Activity 6.9. Be *very* specific. Someone else should be able to use your key without your being there to explain it. Include all necessary instructions to the grader.

Delayed Recall

Though a student may successfully progress through a series of subtasks and demonstrate acquisition of a set of new behaviors on a posttest, this is no guarantee that those behaviors will occur appropriately at some later date. Absence of reinforcement of the new behaviors *(extinction)*, forgetting, or the acquisition of behaviors that interfere with the newly learned behaviors may occur. To evaluate the persistence of learning, a delayed-retention test may be administered. This will usually consist of either the postassessment items or of parallel counterparts to them. (An example of a delayed-retention test is the final exam in a laboratory course.)

Since a delayed-retention evaluation can only occur after a passage of time, you will not be required to implement this aspect of the evaluation program. If you want to assess the staying power of your instruction, giving a delayed-retention test should prove a worthwhile exercise.

6.11   Describe the delayed-evaluation scheme you plan to use. Carry it out and write the results on a separate sheet of paper.

6.12   *Evaluation Procedure Checklist.* Check each item or procedure for these qualities:

   a.   Is the performance evaluated directly specified by or related to the subtask? _____

   b.   If appropriate, are all the situations and items different from the examples used during instruction? _____

c. Are all performances measurable? _____

d. Are the concepts and procedures required the same as those the students practiced? _____

e. Using your observational instructions, would a naive observer score each response exactly as you would? _____

f. Do you have a means of evaluating *every* required *entering behavior* before the lesson? _____

g. Do you have a method for assessing the accomplishment of each requisite response in a student's progress towards accomplishing your enabling objective or subtask? _____

h. Do you have assessment procedures both before and after the lesson for all major subtasks? _____

i. Will you measure the students' ability to perform the major subtasks before—and *all* objective subtasks after or during—the lesson? _____

6.13 If possible, arrange to teach this lesson to an entire class. If you don't have access to a class, choose a sample group of students— one to five subjects of the appropriate age group for the lesson you have designed. If you cannot find subjects of the appropriate age, ask some friends to "role play" your students. Give them some simple instructions for role playing, reminding them that their serious participation is essential. You should have no trouble finding several people willing to help you out. Whom will you teach?

Please look over the evaluation procedure checklist (6.12) carefully before proceeding!

6.14 Administer a short preassessment (the one you designed in 6.8) to your group of students. Attach the results to this page.

6.15 Teach your lesson to the group of students, recording their progress according to the system you planned in Activity 4 (attach progress records).

6.16   Administer your postevaluation as constructed in Activity 6.9. Score it using the method you described in Activity 6.10.

6.17   Discuss the results of the evaluation with your students.

    a.   Write down the numbers of the items they feel need revising, and any suggestions they offer.

_____

_____

_____

_____

    b.   Write down the numbers of the items that many of the students answered incorrectly.

_____

    c.   Revise each item listed in 6.17 a. and 6.17 b., briefly explaining your revision.

_____

_____

_____

_____

_____

_____

6.18 Discuss the instructional procedure with your students. Write down their comments or suggestions. Briefly describe any changes you would make in your instructional sequence in accordance with the results of your evaluation and the student feedback. Remember: the requirement that you revise materials and techniques after they have been tested—trying out procedures until you find those which are demonstrated to be the most effective—is the prime factor that sets this instructional strategy apart from more traditional strategies.

_____

_____

_____

_____

_____

_____

_____

6.19 Show evaluation data to and discuss your instructional procedures with people who observed but did not participate in teaching your lesson—a supervising teacher, principal, or staff supervisor. (If not applicable, write *NA*.) Write their comments here.

_____

_____

_____

_____

Show your instructor any work done by your students that you can bring along.

6.20   *Final Lesson and Evaluation Checklist.* Did you:
Use a class or appropriate sample of subjects? _____
Have the lesson, the materials, the preassessment, and the final evaluation procedure checked by your instructor? _____
Administer a preassessment? _____
Follow your lesson outline? _____
Make any changes in procedure necessitated during the lesson? _____
Administer a final evaluation exam or procedure? _____
Discuss the results of the lesson with your students and your supervisors? _____
Revise preassessment or other evaluations (ongoing, final)? (Attach revisions.) _____
Administer a delayed-retention assessment? _____
Decide on future revisions to the sequence? _____
Consider remedial instruction or additional instruction if necessary? _____

6.21   Write your comments on or suggestions for Activity 6.

_____

_____

_____

_____

_____

_____

_____

_____

_____

_____

6.22 Write your comments on or suggestions for the full sequence of activities in this book.

_____

_____

_____

_____

_____

_____

_____

_____

_____

_____

Congratulations! You have just taken a giant step towards becoming an effective, _accountable_ instructor!

SUPPLEMENTARY EXERCISES

1. Evaluation Systems—School Visit

Purpose: To familiarize you with sample evaluation systems currently in operation.

Arrange with your instructor to visit a school in the vicinity.

1. Plan a meeting with the teacher before visiting a class. Ask the teacher what the goals of instruction are for that particular day, week, or period.

2. Ask the instructor what methods he or she is using to assess the students' entering behaviors and the performance of the students at the end of instruction.

3. Describe and provide samples of teacher-made assessment instruments (quizzes, tests, checklists, charts); provide examples of any published assessment instruments being used.

4. Comment on the reliability of the assessment methods.

5. Comment on the validity of the assessment instruments.

6. Suggest any alternative methods that you think would be appropriate for assessing achievement.

7. Make your own comments and suggestions.

2. Assessment Methods in Published Form

Purpose: To provide you with the experience of reviewing and critically evaluating published assessment methods.

1. Record the following information about any one of the sources listed below.
   a. *Information:*
      - The objectives or student responses being evaluated
      - The reliability of the assessment procedures
      - The validity of the assessment procedures
      - The objectivity of the assessment procedures
      - Any changes that you think would be appropriate in these procedures
   b. *Sources:*
      - Teacher guides and accompanying quizzes or examinations
      - Printed standardized achievement tests, such as those found in individually prescribed instruction
      - Tests that accompany programmed instruction booklets, teaching machine programs, or computer-assisted instruction
      - Teacher-made tests

2. Add your own comments and suggestions.

SUGGESTED READINGS AND REFERENCES

Anastasiow, N. *Educational Psychology: A Contemporary View.* Del Mar., Ca.: Communications Research Machines, 1973. Chapter 18, pp. 363–69 (constructing classroom tests).

Anderson, R. C., and Faust, G. W. *Educational Psychology: The Science of Instruction and Learning.* New York: Dodd, Mead & Co., 1973. Chapter 3, pp. 88–91 (assessing entry level); chapter 4, pp. 125–66 (evaluation—progress tests and posttests; testing for principles and concepts).

Biehler, R. F. *Psychology Applied to Teaching.* Boston: Houghton Mifflin Co., 1971. Chapter 11, pp. 379–97 (characteristics of tests and the construction of tests).

Blair, G. M.; Jones, R.S.; and Simpson, R. H. *Educational Psychology.* New York: Macmillan Co., 1975. Chapter 17, pp. 479–85 (constructing tests).

Bushell, D., Jr. *Classroom Behavior.* Englewood Cliffs, N.J.: Prentice-Hall, 1973. Chapter 3, pp. 35–47 (pretest for entry level; objective progress records; and two types of measurement).

DeCecco, J. P., and Crawford, W. R. *The Psychology of Learning and Instruction.* Englewood Cliffs, N.J.: Prentice-Hall, 1974. Chapter 13, pp. 410–47 (performance assessment).

Hamachek, D. E. *Behavior Dynamics in Teaching, Learning, and Growth.* Boston: Allyn & Bacon, 1975. Chapter 13, pp. 606–18 (ways to plan and construct good classroom tests).

Klausmeier, H. J., and Goodwin, W. *Learning and Human Abilities: Educational Psychology.* 4th ed. New York: Harper & Row, Publishers, 1966. Chapter 17, pp. 437–40 (attributes of good measurement) and pp. 452–61 (teacher-developed procedures for assessment); chapter 18, pp. 465–72 (evaluating student learning and progress).

Lefrancois, G. R. *Psychology for Teaching.* Belmont, Ca.: Wadsworth Publishing Co., 1975. Chapter 13, pp. 276–85 (teacher-made tests).

Thorndike, R. L. *Educational Measurement.* 2nd ed. Washington, D.C.: American Council on Education, 1971.

AFTERWORD

Now that you have completed the manual, you have practiced a complete set of basic procedures that contribute to effective instruction. You have acquired a new set of behaviors which will be useful to you in the future, and which you may want to refine or refresh once in a while. Although the flow diagram of figure 1 may be all you need, a more detailed outline is provided here. It should help you remember how to sequence the steps to effectively construct, administer, and evaluate an instructional sequence. If you feel you need any more direction with any of these steps, simply select the activity or activities you need and review them separately. For additional information or practice, refer to the "Suggested Readings and References" for the activity you are reviewing.

We hope you will use this outline often, adding to and modifying it to fit your special needs. Perhaps it will make the task of bridging the gap between theory and practice a little easier and a lot more fun.

OUTLINE OF THE GENERAL INSTRUCTIONAL MODEL

I. **Define Objectives**
   A. List educational goals that are
      1. challenging
      2. interesting
      3. relevant

      and select one to serve as the focus of your instruction.
   B. Write instructional objectives that relate to the educational goal, including:
      1. observable behavior written as an action verb
      2. conditions
      3. a standard or criterion

      and select one of these objectives.

II. **Analyze Task**
   A. Break down the instructional objective into its component enabling objectives and subtasks
   B. Make an outline or flow diagram of the logical ordering of subtasks (a task analysis)
   C. Check to be sure you have selected relevant and sophisticated subtasks
      1. Include relevant cognitive, affective, and psychomotor behavior
      2. Include all appropriate levels of cognitive behavior

III. **Determine Entering Behavior**
   A. Specify the neccesary entering behaviors for the instruction you plan to design
   B. Describe student characteristics that may affect entering behavior, including:
      1. communication skills
      2. social skills
      3. learning-facilitation skills
   C. Assess prerequisite behaviors
   D. Adjust instruction to disparities between student behavioral repertoires and requisite entering behaviors
   E. Design procedures responsive to individual differences of students in group

IV. **Plan Recording, Feedback, and Management Procedures**
   A. List all performances to be recorded as the student progresses
   B. Decide on methods for assessing accomplishments of these tasks

    C. Set up a record-keeping and feedback system that:
1. is simple to use
2. records small steps
3. allows for frequent evaluation
4. provides a complete picture of all desired performances
5. is readily accessible to students
6. employs active student participation
7. provides an appropriate guideline for students to gauge their progress
8. is appropriate to the interests and developmental levels of your students

    D. Select procedures for classroom management that include:
1. reinforcing correct student responses
2. avoiding problem behaviors
3. coping with problem behaviors

V. Develop Instruction

    A. Choose specific materials and procedures to use in your instruction

    B. Consider alternative formats

    C. Design a sequence that employs:
1. logical sequencing
2. relevant and effective instructional stimuli
3. active student involvement
4. appropriate feedback
5. reinforced progress

VI. Implement Instruction, Evaluate Its Effectiveness, and Revise Your Lesson

    A. Check final form of instructional objective, enabling objective(s), subtask(s), and methods of assessing their accomplishment

    B. Design an evaluation system measuring:
1. entering behaviors
2. subtasks and enabling behaviors
3. progress through task completion
4. terminal behaviors as specified in your objective
5. delayed retention

    C. Verify that your evaluation system is:
1. valid
2. reliable
3. objective

    D. Construct answer keys or criteria lists capable of independent use by another staff member or by the student

    E. Administer instruction and evaluation as planned

    F. Obtain feedback from students and/or supervisors

    G. Modify instructional plan accordingly

VII. Pat yourself on the back and tell someone else about what you've accomplished!

ABOUT THE AUTHORS

Beth Sulzer-Azaroff has taught, served as consultant, and conducted research in inner-city schools, institutions for the retarded, clinics, and universities. After receiving her Ph.D. at the University of Minnesota, she taught at Southern Illinois University. Currently a professor of psychology at the University of Massachusetts, she teaches educational psychology and applied behavior analysis. In addition to actively serving on the editorial staffs of several major behavior journals, she has recently published two books with G. R. Mayer: *Behavior Modification Procedures for School Personnel* and *Applying Behavior Analysis Procedures with Children and Youth.*

Judy McKinley Brewer received her B.A. in psychology at the University of California at Los Angeles and her M.S. and Ph.D. in cognitive psychology at the University of Massachusetts. She is currently research coordinator and program specialist for the Mansfield Day Treatment Center in Connecticut, which offers a comprehensive psychoeducational program for functionally retarded children with severe behavior disorders.

Linda Ford has a B.S. from the University of Massachusetts and presently is program director for the day treatment program of First Few Steps, Inc. This organization helps adults to return from restrictive settings to the mainstream environment by helping them develop self-sufficiency and independence.